Rebecca Parkinson is a trained te
children's worker and published a
four years at primary level before becoming a teacher adviser
for Lancashire and working alongside Lancashire Business and
Enterprise Team to develop curriculum-based Road Show packages
for Early Years and KS1 and 2. She has lectured part-time at
Liverpool University as a PGCE course tutor and currently teaches
part-time as well as giving one-to-one tuition in Maths and Literacy
up to GCSE level.

Rebecca has also been involved in two separate projects that
gave her the opportunity to work with teachers in local schools and
youth clubs in Romania and Indonesia. Rebecca is the author of
the '12 Hidden Heroes' series published by Day One Publications
and she writes regular resources for the SPCK assemblies website.
She lives in Lancashire with her husband and two children and is
an active member of her local Free Methodist Church, where she
runs the youth and children's work with her husband.

Barnabas
for
Children®

Barnabas for Children® is a registered word mark and the logo is a registered device mark of The Bible Reading Fellowship.

Text copyright © Rebecca Parkinson 2012
The author asserts the moral right
to be identified as the author of this work

Published by
The Bible Reading Fellowship
15 The Chambers, Vineyard
Abingdon OX14 3FE
United Kingdom
Tel: +44 (0)1865 319700
Email: enquiries@brf.org.uk
Website: www.brf.org.uk
BRF is a Registered Charity

ISBN 978 0 85746 004 2

First published 2012
10 9 8 7 6 5 4 3 2 1 0

Acknowledgments
Unless otherwise stated, scripture quotations are taken from the Contemporary English Version of the Bible published by HarperCollins Publishers, copyright © 1991, 1992, 1995 American Bible Society.

The paper used in the production of this publication was supplied by mills that source their raw materials from sustainably managed forests. Soy-based inks were used in its printing and the laminate film is biodegradable.

A catalogue record for this book is available from the British Library

Printed in Singapore by Craft Print International Ltd

FILL THE GAP!

120 instant **Bible games** for
Sunday schools and midweek groups

Rebecca Parkinson

✱ For the Junior Church team at Fulwood Free Methodist Church, who work so hard to make a difference to children's lives. Also for the many children who have tried and tested the games in this book. ✱

Acknowledgments

As I grew up, I was fortunate to have many people who took the time to make church interesting and relevant. I would like to thank them for all they did and for the difference they made to so many of our lives. As an adult it has been a privilege to work with many children in schools and churches. I would like to thank them all for their enthusiasm and the joy they have given me.

Thanks to Ted, Anna and Lydia for their ideas and encouragement. Thanks to Joanne for all the suggestions and for coming up with the rhymes for the story of Paul's shipwreck. Thank you also to Sue Doggett for editing the manuscript.

I would particularly like to thank my mum, not only for all her suggestions but also for the hours she has spent checking my work.

*

CONTENTS

Games for Old Testament stories

Creation

Adam and Eve

Noah

Abraham and Sarah

Isaac and Rebekah

Games for New Testament stories

The early Church

Dorcas

Paul and Silas

Shipwreck

The Bible

*

FOREWORD

Jesus said, 'I promise you this. If you don't change and become like a child, you will never get into the kingdom of heaven' (Matthew 18:3).

We are called to this childlikeness, but it takes greater spiritual insight and communication skills to carry great truths of the Bible to small children, I would say, than to almost any other audience in the world.

The fundamental needs of children are moral and intimately related to the gospel, and the way they discover, create and understand is something that the church needs to really engage with, to communicate the story to the next generation. In this respect, children brought up in our most visually sophisticated age need creative, dynamic, participative material. Rebecca, with her expertise, creativity and scriptural basis, provides a fantastic opportunity for children to engage with scripture so that it becomes a part of their everyday lives.

When we understand the preciousness of children and their ability to grasp things in a way that others often don't, we will provide some amazing tools with which they can live their lives. Rebecca has sought to achieve such a goal with clear objectives, starting with the Bible, releasing creativity and engaging in a relevant way to different age groups.

For anyone engaged in children's ministry, this will provide a fantastic resource, and I want to affirm anyone in children's ministry to see the potential of that transformation happening in children's lives.

Roy Crowne, Executive Director, HOPE
www.hopetogether.org.uk / www.hope-revolution.com

*

INTRODUCTION

If you have ever needed a time-filler because a church service has overrun or your session has finished too early... felt that you wanted to include a fun element to your session but been unsure what to do... looked in a games book and been overwhelmed by the amount of equipment needed for every game... then *Fill the Gap!* is for you!

Fill the Gap! covers 60 well-known Bible stories and suggests two games for each story, one aimed at younger children aged 4–7 and the other at older children aged 8–11 years. Each game is designed to bring a fun element to every Bible story, to help children remember what they have learnt. Many of the games can be easily adapted to fit different Bible stories (see 'Helpful hints').

The ideas have been designed to be quick and easy to use. The games are clearly presented so that the book can be taken off the shelf and a game read and played immediately. The games have been tried and tested by children's and youth workers and are a great way of reinforcing a teaching point.

Health and safety

The safety of the children is of utmost importance when playing games. It is recommended that you check the room for potential hazards, such as stacked chairs, trailing cables or unobserved exits, before any game is played, but particularly when high-energy games are being used. It is also recommended that less physical games are played if there is a wide age range of children involved (see 'Age bandings' below).

Group sizes

Most of the games in this book are suitable for both smaller and larger groups of children. For large groups, it is suggested that more teams are used rather than having large numbers of children in each team. It is hoped that leaders will join in with the games and will make up numbers where necessary.

Age bandings

The age bandings given in this book are only suggestions. Most games can be modified slightly to make them appropriate for older or younger children. Where children of mixed ages are playing a game, particular care should be taken of the safety of the younger children; it is suggested that less physical games are used with younger children. For groups with a wide age range, the most suitable game relating to each story is also noted as 'All ages'. In some cases, both games are appropriate for mixed age ranges and are therefore both noted as such.

Commonly used objects

Most of the games need no equipment. On the occasions when a resource is required, it is always an item that is easily available in most places. Below is a list of equipment that is occasionally required. It is recommended that you prepare a 'ready box' so that the resources are available at short notice.

- paper or card
- pencils
- blindfold (scarf)

- music (CD and CD player or MP3 player, docking station and suitable downloads)
- sticky tape
- chairs
- two pairs of large socks
- scissors
- something with which to mark start and finish lines, such as chairs, masking tape, or chalk
- a coin
- a watch, clock, or mobile phone to time seconds
- a small ball or beanbag

GAMES FOR
OLD TESTAMENT
STORIES

✱

CREATION

Story reference: Genesis 1:1—2:3

Creation corners

Age banding
4–7 (Reception to Year 3)
All ages

Aim
To help children learn the days of creation; to reinforce the story of creation and to emphasise that God made everything.

You will need
A blindfold for the leader (optional); music CD and CD player (optional); some pictures drawn quickly and simply on pieces of paper (you could write the words for older children).

The pictures can show anything that God created, such as different animals or different flowers. Alternatively, they can show the days of creation. For example:

- Day 1: Light and dark
- Day 2: Sky and water
- Day 3: Plants
- Day 4: Sun, moon, stars
- Day 5: Fish and birds
- Day 6: Animals and people

How to play

Place the pictures of things that God created around the room. Explain that when you ask them to, everyone will choose one of the pictures and stand next to it. (You may like to play music while the children are moving.) One leader should be blindfolded or should look away from the children as they move. When all the children have chosen their picture, the music stops and the leader shouts out the name of one of the pictures without looking.

If you want an overall winner, all the children standing at the picture that is called are out and sit down. The children remaining repeat the game; each time, those standing at the picture that is called sit down. Eventually there will be only one child remaining— the winner.

If you want all the children to join in the game the whole time, all the children standing at the picture that is called are declared the winners of that round and everyone has another go.

Helpful hint

This game can be played to reinforce any Bible story by renaming the corners: for example, the tribes of Israel, names of prophets, Jesus' miracles and so on.

God made...

Age banding
7–11 (Years 3 to 6)

Aim
To help the children learn the days of creation.

You will need
No equipment is needed.

How to play
Explain the following actions to the children.

Day 1: Light and dark
Grab a partner and sit facing each other. One child covers their eyes for darkness and the other lifts their head and opens their arms to indicate light.

Day 2: Water
Lie flat on the floor on your back.

Day 3: Plants
Stand upright, with arms outstretched like a tree.

Day 4: Sun, moon, stars
Star jumps.

Day 5: Fish and birds
Flap like a fish or bird.

Day 6: Animals and people

Grab a partner. One child kneels down on all fours; the other pets the first child.

Shout out the descriptions listed above, allowing enough time for the children to respond to each call. For example, 'Water!' (all the children quickly lie on the floor); 'Sun, moon and stars!' (the children do star jumps until the next instruction is given). Gradually get quicker with the instructions, and try to alternate standing-up actions with those that are on the floor.

This game needs to be played quickly. By the end of the game, the children should be out of breath. The game can just be played for fun or the last child to do an action can be out, repeating until a winner is found.

Helpful hint

When the children have firmly grasped the game, you may like to shout out 'Day 1', 'Day 5' and so on rather than the words 'Light and dark' or 'Animals and people'.

*

ADAM AND EVE

Story reference: Genesis 2:4—3:24

Snaking around!

Age banding
4–7 (Reception to Year 3)

Aim
To remind the children that Eve listened to what the snake said and disobeyed God. This meant that people couldn't be close friends with God any more.

You will need
Chairs to act as simple obstacles.

How to play
Ask all the children to line up behind a leader. To get them warmed up, ask each one to hold on to the waist of the child in front, with the front child holding the leader's waist. The leader now leads them round the room, in and out between the obstacles, twisting and turning like a snake squirming across the floor. The children must not let go of each other and must follow the leader wherever he or she goes.

Explain that the leader is going to repeat the above, but this time he or she is going to do actions that the children have to copy. The children must always keep hold of the child in front with at least one hand.

For example, the leader may hop on one leg; the children must try to do the same while holding on to the chain. The leader may tap his head with one hand; the children must try to tap their own head while keeping hold of the child in front with their other hand.

When the children have got used to the game, allow one of them to go at the front of the 'snake' and make up actions for everyone to follow.

Helpful hint

Don't let the leading child move too quickly. Emphasise that it is the actions that are important, not the speed at which the children move.

Tempting keys

Age banding

7–11 (Years 3 to 6)
All ages

Aim

To remind the children that when we do wrong things, we often sneak around in the hope that no one will notice what we have done.

You will need

Car keys on a keyring (the larger the bunch, the better); a blindfold.

How to play

Ask the children to sit in a circle, with one child sitting cross-legged in the middle. Spread the circle out so that there is a reasonable distance between the child in the centre and those in the circle.

Place some keys on the floor in front of the central child and cover the child's eyes with a blindfold. Explain that you will point to a child in the circle, who must then tiptoe forward and pick up the keys without the child in the middle noticing. If the central child hears anyone approaching, they must point in the direction of the noise. If they point directly at the 'robber', the 'robber' must return to his or her place and another child will be selected to try to take the keys. If the robber succeeds in stealing the keys, he or she replaces the central child, who moves into the circle.

Helpful hint

If no keys are available, a shaker, a screwed-up plastic bag, a packet of crisps, or anything that makes a noise when touched, can be used.

---

*

NOAH

Story reference: Genesis 6:1—9:17

Listen to Noah

Age banding
4–7 (Reception to Year 3)

Aim
To remind the children that Noah took lots of animals into the ark.

You will need
No equipment is needed.

How to play
This game is similar to the well-known game 'Simon says'. Explain to the children that they are all going to pretend to be animals. Check that the children know what noises a variety of well-known animals make. Explain that they must only do as you tell them when you say the words 'Noah says...' before your command.

For example:

- **Noah says 'dogs'**: the children should bark.
- **Noah says 'cats'**: the children should meow.
- **Noah says 'cows'**: the children should moo.
- **'Dogs'**: the children should do nothing.
- **'Horses'**: the children should do nothing.

When the children have got used to following these instructions, the game can be made more active by adding further instructions. For example:

- **Noah says 'act like a duck':** the children should waddle around the room.
- **Noah says 'act like a snake':** the children should wriggle on the floor.
- **Noah says 'act like an elephant':** the children should move around using their arms as trunks.
- **'Act like a monkey':** the children should do nothing.

The game can be simply played for fun or children can be asked to move to the side if they make an incorrect action or noise.

Helpful hints

- With younger children, the game works best if three or four animals are selected and the actions or noises repeated. Using too many animals can confuse them.
- Rather than asking the children to sit still if they are 'out', ask them to move to one side and continue to join in.

Noisy animals

Age banding
7–11 (Years 3 to 6)
All ages

Aim
To remind the children of the variety of animals that Noah took into the ark.

You will need

CD and CD player (optional); small pieces of paper for animal families to be written on.

Each animal name needs to be written on four pieces of paper. For example:

cow   cow   cow   cow   horse   horse   horse   horse

dog   dog   dog   dog   pig   pig   pig   pig

You will need the same number of pieces of paper as there are people playing. It is also important that there is the same number of each animal, so leaders may need to take part to make up the numbers.

How to play

Give each child a piece of paper with an animal name written on it and ask them to fold it up. Explain that when the music starts, the children need to keep swapping their folded piece of paper with as many others as possible. When the music stops, the children quickly undo the paper in their hand, read what animal is written on the paper and immediately make the noise of their animal as loudly as they can.

The aim of the game is for the children to find the other members of their animal 'family' by the noise that they make. For example, if a child's paper has the word 'cow' on it, they will walk around 'mooing' until they have found the other three children making the same noise. When they have found their 'family', all four children sit on each other's knees on a chair, with the biggest at the bottom, going up to the smallest on the top.

The winner is the family that is the first to be piled up in order. The children then fold up their papers and play again.

Helpful hints

- If you have not already prepared this game, split the children into groups of four and ask each group to write a specific animal name on four pieces of paper. Make sure each group has chosen a different animal. Then continue as above.
- If recorded music is not available, clap your hands while the children swap papers and shout 'stop' when ready.

*

ABRAHAM AND SARAH

Story reference: Genesis 18:1–15

Announcements

Age banding
4–7 (Reception to Year 3)
All ages

Aim
To remind children that Sarah laughed when she heard the visitors' message.

You will need
No equipment is needed.

How to play
Mark a start line on the floor and line the children up in teams behind this line. Place a chair opposite each team at the other end of the room. There should be as many chairs as there are teams.

Explain that the first child in each team is going to have a message whispered to them. The child then has to run from the start line, round the chair and back to the start line, and whisper the message to the next child. The second child repeats the process to the third child. The game continues until each child has 'taken the message' and passed it on to the next person. When the last team member returns to the start line, he or she must whisper the correct message to the leader and then the whole team sits down.

The winning team is the team that is sitting down first and gets the message correct.

The leader should tell the children the original message and see if anyone passed it on correctly. Usually the messages received are very different from the original and the children think it is extremely funny.

Helpful hints

- Make sure the first child does not tell the others in the line what the original message was.
- Use this game to pass on a current piece of news to the children, such as 'Tomorrow it is Lauren's birthday', or 'Sophie and Sam have just got engaged', or 'Anna has a new baby sister called Lydia.'

Knowing Abraham

Age banding
7–11 (Years 3 to 6)

Aim
To help the children become familiar with words associated with the story of Abraham.

You will need

Small pieces of paper with words written on them, relating to the story of Abraham (for example, Abraham, Sarah, Ur, Haran, Canaan, Egypt, Isaac, Lot, covenant, Terah, stars, sheep, altar, descendants, promise); chairs.

How to play
Place the chairs in a circle facing inwards and ask the children to sit on them. There should be one chair fewer than the number of children. Ask the child without a chair to stand in the centre of the circle.

Give each child a slip of paper with one of the words about Abraham on it. The child in the centre also needs a slip of paper. If there are lots of children, the words can be duplicated, with two children being given the same word.

Shout out two of the words, followed by the word 'change'—for example, 'Abraham and Canaan... change.' On the word 'change', Abraham and Canaan try to swap seats, but the child in the middle of the circle tries to sit on one of the vacated chairs before the others can swap. Whichever child ends up without a chair stands in the middle while another pair is called out. The process is then repeated.

As the game progresses, three or four words can be shouted out before the 'change' order is given. If the instruction 'all change' is shouted, all the children need to swap seats and the child in the middle tries to find a free place.

Helpful hints

- Write the words you are using on a piece of paper so that you can tick them off as you call them out. This way, all the children will get a fair number of turns rather than one child having lots of turns and others none.
- This game can be played to reinforce any Bible story. For example, the words could be the tribes of Israel, names of prophets, Jesus' disciples and so on.

*

ISAAC AND REBEKAH

Story reference: Genesis 24

Catching Isaac

Age banding
4–7 (Reception to Year 3)

Aim
To remind the children of the way in which Isaac and Rebekah met.

You will need
The tune for the children's song 'In and out the bluebell windows'.

How to play
The game begins with two leaders facing each other and joining hands to form an archway. (Children can make the archway if not enough adults are available.) Teach the children the first verse of the song to the tune 'In and out the bluebell windows'.

Verse 1
We've been learning about Isaac
We've been learning about Isaac
We've been learning about Isaac
Can we catch an Isaac?

Ask the children to form a line. Explain that, as they sing the song, the children are all going to pass under the archway and then join the back of the queue. When the last line of the song arrives, the leaders will bring their arms down to catch someone on the word 'Isaac'. This child will then lead the procession under the archway until the next verse is complete.

Verse 2
Isaac's servant's at the well
Isaac's servant's at the well
Isaac's servant's at the well
Can we catch a servant?

The leaders bring down their arms on the word 'servant' and catch another child. The servant is placed behind Isaac and the game continues, singing Verses 3 and 4 until Rebekah and Abraham have been caught.

Verse 3
Can we find a wife for Isaac?
Can we find a wife for Isaac?
Can we find a wife for Isaac?
Can we catch Rebekah?

Verse 4
We are going home to Abraham
We are going home to Abraham
We are going home to Abraham
Can we catch an Abraham?

For the last verse, Isaac and Rebekah, and the servant and Abraham, make two further archways for the remaining children to pass under so that three wedding guests are 'caught'.

Verse 5
Who is going to the wedding?
Who is going to the wedding?
Who is going to the wedding?
Can we catch the guests?

Depending on the number of children present, the wedding guests could then make further arches to 'catch' other children as Verse 5 is repeated.

Helpful hint

If the tune for 'In and out the bluebell windows' is unknown, simply using the verses as a chant will work well.

Rebekah's skill

Age banding
7–11 (Years 3 to 6)
All ages

Aim
To remind the children that Isaac's servant realised that Rebekah was the person he was looking for when she gave him some water.

You will need

Plastic cups or rolled cones of paper (if cups are not available).

How to play

Split the children into teams of approximately six players. Mark a starting and finishing line on the floor and ask the teams to line up behind the starting line.

Give each team a cup. Explain that the first child will balance the cup on their head (without holding it), move to the finishing line, turn round, move back to the starting line and pass the cup to the next person. If the cup falls off, they pick it up and continue from where it dropped. The first team to have each person complete the task and be sitting down is the winner.

Variations of the game could include crawling on all fours with the cup balanced on their back, or seeing who can stand on one leg for the longest with the cup balanced on their head. If the weather is good and you don't mind the children getting wet, the game could be played outside, with the children having to transport water in the cups in their hands to a container at the finishing line. The team that transports the most water wins.

Helpful hint

The idea of this game is to imagine Rebekah carrying the jars on her head, so, if plastic cups are not available, books, paper plates or any similar objects could be used.

---

*

JACOB AND ESAU

Story reference: Genesis 27

Feely game

Age banding
4–7 (Reception to Year 3)

Aim
To help the children understand how Isaac was tricked into believing that Jacob was actually his brother Esau.

You will need
Socks (or bags) with objects inside; some simple, non-breakable everyday objects, such as a spoon, rubber, key, toothbrush, comb and so on.

How to play
Place one object into each sock and tie the ends of the socks so that the children can't see inside. Give each child a sock and see if they can guess what is inside it. Older children can be given a piece of paper numbered from 1 to 10 (or however many items you have used), so that they can secretly fill in the answers. Younger children will just enjoy the fun of guessing. If the game finishes too early, ask a few children to go and find an object to place in a sock for the other children to guess.

Helpful hint

If socks or bags are not available, the objects can be placed behind a screen (such as an open book or piece of card) and the children can be asked to reach round the screen to feel the objects.

Guess who?

Age banding

7–11 (Years 3 to 6)
All ages

Aim

To help the children understand how Isaac was tricked into believing that Jacob was actually his brother Esau, as they explore the importance of touch, sight and sound.

You will need

Chairs; a blindfold; pencils and paper; a screen or a doorway.

How to play

Arrange the chairs in a circle facing inwards, with one chair in the middle. Ask all the children to sit on a chair and then blindfold one of the children. When you point to a child in the circle, he or she has to go and sit on the central chair. The blindfolded child is then led to the central chair and has to guess who is sitting on the chair, by touch. When they have guessed correctly, the person on the chair becomes blindfolded and another child is chosen to sit in the centre.

Alternatively, split the group in half and ask each half to write down the names of the children in the opposite half. (This could be done by a leader, writing the names on a large board for all the children to see.) Ask the children to have a good look at one another, as they are going to need to have been observant.

Take half of the children behind a screen or out of the room and ask the remaining half to sit down and write down 1 to whatever number of children have just left the group. For example, if six children have left the room, write down 1–6; if ten children have left, write down 1–10, and so on. Explain that, in turn, each child behind the screen is going to stick out their hand so that the seated children can see it. The seated children then have to guess whose hand it is and write down the name. This could be done individually, in pairs or even as a group.

Make sure the children showing their hands stay in the same order for marking the results. When each child has 'shown their hand', ask them to do so again, but this time also to show the 'guessers' who the hand belongs to. A lot of the answers will probably be wrong!

Swap the groups over, but this time ask the children to remove their shoes and socks and show their feet before repeating the game. The game can be carried out using hands, feet, knees or elbows, and also works with a slit cut in a sheet for looking at each other's eyes.

Helpful hint

Sometimes children can be embarrassed by showing their socks (they may have holes in them or have forgotten to wash them). Be sensitive and allow the children to leave their shoes on if necessary, or even let the children decide if they want to show their hands instead.

*

JOSEPH: HIS DAD'S FAVOURITE

Story reference: Genesis 37

Joseph is missing

Age banding
4–7 (Reception to Year 3)
All ages

Aim
To remind the children that Jacob gave Joseph a special coat to show how much he loved him, but the brothers were jealous and got rid of Joseph.

You will need

A large piece of material or a large coat (multi-coloured material is best).

How to play
Ask the children to have a good look round at the other children present in the room. Leaders should also be included, especially if numbers are small. Explain that one child is going to leave the room and that the remaining children are going to move around and then sit down on the floor. The teacher will then cover one of the seated children with the piece of material or a coat. The child

who has left the room will now be asked to return and to guess which child has 'gone missing' (under the cloth).

The game can be repeated with different children leaving the room.

Helpful hint

This is a good game for including children who struggle to join in. They often enjoy being covered with the cloth.

Escape the pit

Age banding

7–11 (Years 3 to 6)

Aim

To remind the children that Joseph's brothers were jealous of him, so they threw him down a pit.

You will need

Chairs.

How to play

Ask each child to place a chair in a circle facing inwards and sit on it. Make sure the chairs are as close together as possible. Ask one child to stand in the middle, leaving his or her chair empty. Explain that the child in the middle is 'Joseph' and the circle of chairs is the pit that his brothers threw him into.

The aim of the game is for 'Joseph' to sit on the free chair and thus 'escape'. However, to stop the escape, all the children are going to shuffle clockwise round the circle of chairs, sitting in the free chair as it becomes available. Joseph will have to move quickly to find a free chair. If he or she manages to sit on a free chair, the child on the right of that chair moves into the middle. If having only one free chair proves too difficult, a second free chair may be added.

Helpful hint

This game can be played to reinforce many Bible stories—for example, Jonah escaping from the mouth of the large fish, Daniel in the lions' den, Jeremiah down the pit and so on.

*

JOSEPH: DREAMS, PROMOTION, REUNION

Story reference: Genesis 40—46

Interpretation

Age banding
4–7 (Reception to Year 3)

Aim
To remind the children that God gave Joseph the ability to interpret dreams.

<table>
<tr><td>You will need</td></tr>
<tr><td>A list of actions for the children to perform (see below).</td></tr>
</table>

How to play
Remind the children that Joseph had to ask God to help him understand the meaning of Pharaoh's dreams. Explain that they are going to have a go at interpreting someone's actions. Ask the children to sit on the floor and ask one child to come forward. Whisper an action to the child and help him or her act out the action so that the other children can guess what they are doing.

Actions could include:

- making a bed
- making a sandwich

- being a doctor
- being a dog
- ballet dancing
- riding a bike
- having a shower
- swimming
- playing football
- having an argument
- being a teacher
- being an elephant
- washing up
- wrapping a present
- putting up an umbrella
- playing tennis
- driving a car
- hammering some wood

When someone guesses correctly, they come forward and a different action is whispered to them. If children are too shy to carry out an action on their own, they could act in pairs or even be given a small amount of time to work out a group action, such as saving a goal at a football match.

Helpful hint

Some children will like to make up their own actions to act out. If they want to do this, ask them to whisper what they are doing to you first, so that you can help them if necessary.

Giant pairs

Age banding
7–11 (Years 3 to 6)
All ages

Aim
To remind the children about different aspects of the story of Joseph.

You will need

A board or large piece of paper; pieces of A4 card or paper (all the same colour and size); pencils.

How to play
On a board or large piece of paper, make a list with the children of any words they can think of relating to the story of Joseph—for example, dream, Pharaoh, Potiphar, personal servant, chef, prison, corn, cows, pit, brothers, Egypt, barns, famine and so on. (This is a good way to revise the story.)

Give each child two pieces of paper. Ask each child to select one word from your list and write it on one side of both pieces of paper, making both pieces look as identical as possible. If there is time, the children may like to decorate the paper with simple pictures or even simply draw pictures rather than writing the words. Collect all the papers and muddle them up thoroughly.

Split the children into teams of approximately four. Spread all the papers face down on the floor. Ask the teams to position themselves round the edges.

Explain that the game is similar to 'Pairs', which will be familiar to many of them. The first team chooses two pieces of paper to turn over. If they are a pair, the team keeps them and has another go. If the two pieces chosen are not a pair, they are placed back on the floor and the second team has a go. The winner is the team with the most pairs at the end of the game.

Helpful hints

- If paper is being used, give the children pencils to write with, as felt-tip pen will show through on the other side.
- This game can be played to reinforce any Bible story: simply use words relating to a different story rather than words associated with Joseph.

*

MOSES: BIRTH TO BURNING BUSH

Story reference: Exodus 2—3

Where is the baby?

Age banding

4–7 (Reception to Year 3)

Aim

To help the children remember that the Israelites had to keep their babies hidden away because of Pharaoh's threat to kill all the baby boys.

You will need

A small toy figure (Playmobil® or Lego®) or a small figure made out of pipe cleaners or a cardboard cut-out figure. If time allows, the figure could be wrapped in tissue to look like a baby and could even be placed in a pipe-cleaner basket.

How to play

Ask all the children to leave the room while a leader hides the small 'baby' somewhere in the room. The 'baby' should not be too difficult to find, and the children should be told which areas they are not allowed to search, such as cupboards, drawers and so on. When a child finds the 'baby', the other children leave the room while the child hides the figure again, and so the game continues. (**NB:** Be aware of food allergies when using foodstuffs.)

Helpful hint

This game is always popular when Jelly Babies are used rather than a small figure. If Jelly Babies are hidden, then the child eats the Jelly Baby and hides a different one. For cleanliness, sweets should be wrapped in tissue.

Who looked in the basket?

Age banding
7–11 (Years 3 to 6)
All ages

Aim
To help the children remember that Moses was placed in a basket and then found by Pharaoh's daughter.

You will need

Something to represent a basket, such as a bag or box; time to explain how to 'guess correctly' to another leader.

How to play
Ask the children to sit in a circle facing inwards, with a 'basket' placed in the centre.

Explain that a leader is going to go out of the room. You will choose one child, who will stand up, walk to the basket, look in the basket and return to his or her seat. The leader will then come back into the room and you will ask them to correctly guess who looked in the basket.

You are going to point to a child and say, 'Was it (name)?' The 'guesser' will then say 'yes' or 'no'. You again ask, 'Was it (name)?' The guesser will again say 'yes' or 'no'. This continues until the guesser correctly says 'yes'.

Before the game, you should have secretly explained to the guesser that, as they exit the room, they should clearly place a certain number of fingers on the door or wall, indicating to you which child you name will be the one who looked in the basket. This way the guesser should always be correct.

If the guesser places a full hand on the door, the child who looked in the basket will be the fifth child you name. If the guesser places three fingers on the door, the third child you name will have looked in the basket.

For example, the guesser places a full hand on the door, indicating that the fifth child named will have looked in the basket. They then leave the room.

A child (Reanne) is selected to look in the basket; the guesser returns to the room. You ask the guesser, 'Was it Laura?' and the guesser replies, 'No.' 'Was it Oliver?' The guesser replies, 'No.' 'Was it Harriet?' The guesser replies, 'No.' 'Was it James?' The guesser replies, 'No.' 'Was it Reanne?' The guesser replies, 'Yes.'

The children are amazed that the guesser is correct every time!

After a few turns, the children will want to have a go themselves to see if they can guess correctly.

Helpful hint

It is up to you whether you eventually tell the children how it is done. You may like to ask them to think about it and promise to tell them when they return the following week.

*

MOSES: ESCAPE FROM EGYPT

Story reference: Exodus 12:31—14:31

In the Red Sea

Age banding
4–7 (Reception to Year 3)

Aim
To remind the children that God divided the Red Sea so that the Israelites could escape from the Egyptians.

<table>
<tr><td>You will need</td></tr>
<tr><td>No equipment is needed.</td></tr>
</table>

How to play
Mark a line on the floor long enough for all the children to fit along its length. (Several shorter lines are fine if the space is limited.) Explain to the children that one side of the line is the bank of the Red Sea and the other is the actual Red Sea. (You may like to mark the Red Sea with a piece of blue paper to remind the children which side is which.) When you say 'In the sea', the children should jump on to the sea side of the line. When you say 'On the bank', the children should jump on to the bank side of the line. If you say 'On the sea' or 'In the bank', the children should

ignore you. Repeating 'In the sea' or 'On the bank' more than once catches the children out and makes the game more fun.

As the children get used to the game, you can say the instructions more quickly. The game can be played just for fun or the children can be called 'out' if they follow an instruction incorrectly or are too slow.

Helpful hint

When the children have grasped the game as a larger group, you may like to split them into smaller groups of approximately six, and ask them to play the game themselves. The children take it in turns to give the orders.

Moses, Moses, may we cross the deep Red Sea?

Age banding
7–11 (Years 3 to 6)
All ages

Aim
To remind the children that God performed a great miracle when he divided the Red Sea.

You will need

No equipment is needed.

How to play

Mark two lines on the floor at least five metres apart. Divide the children into two teams and position one team behind each line, facing into the middle. Choose one child to be Moses and ask him or her to stand in the middle.

Moses

The children behind both lines say together, 'Moses, Moses, may we cross the deep Red Sea?' The child in the middle (Moses) shouts, 'Only if you are (wearing)...' and the gap may be filled in by saying 'trainers', 'a hair bobble', a particular colour, and so on. For example: 'Only if you are wearing trainers'; 'Only if you are wearing something red'; 'Only if you are a girl'; 'Only if you are six years old'.

The children to whom the instruction refers must then try to cross the sea. The child in the middle has to try to catch them as they cross. The first person to be caught becomes Moses and the process is repeated.

The game can be played with all the children who are caught joining Moses in the middle. For this version to work, a lot more room is needed. The game can also be played with helpers joining Moses in the middle so that more children are caught.

Helpful hint

It is best to have no more than four people in the middle, especially if space is limited. Once this number has been exceeded, you may like to start again with a different Moses.

---

*

JOSHUA: SPIES

Story reference: Numbers 13—14

Carry the grapes

Age banding
4–7 (Reception to Year 3)

Aim
To remind the children that Moses asked the spies to bring back samples of the food they found in Canaan to show him. The clusters of grapes were so big that two people were needed to carry them.

You will need
Two strips of paper (cut a piece of A4 paper lengthways, producing two strips approximately 30cm x 10cm); grapes (about 20). If the game is prepared in advance, it is great played with real grapes. However, it is easy to make grape-sized balls out of screwed-up paper. An A4 sheet will make about six 'grapes'.

How to play
Split the children into two teams, standing behind a start line. Place a chair opposite each team.

𝍌𝍌𝍌𝍌𝍌   chair

𝍌𝍌𝍌𝍌𝍌   chair

Place the piles of grapes at the start line. Place one of the paper strips next to the grapes. Explain that when you say 'Go', the first two children in each team must each take hold of one end of the strip of paper. A team-mate places one grape on the strip and, together, the two 'carriers' must move to the chair and place the grape on the chair. They then run back to the start line and hand the strip to the next pair of children, who repeat the process.

If the grape is dropped on the way to the chair, it is left on the floor, the carriers immediately return to their team and the next two children have a go. The children continue to take turns until all the grapes have been moved from the start line.

At the end of the game, the grapes on the chairs are counted and the team that has successfully transferred the most grapes is declared the winner. If both teams have transported the same number of grapes, the team that finished first is the winner.

Helpful hint

To make the game easier for younger children, use wider strips of paper. To make the game more difficult, use thinner strips, so that the children have to work together even more carefully.

Bring me...

Age banding

7–11 (Years 3 to 6)
All ages

Aim

To remind the children that Moses asked the spies to bring back samples of the food they found in Canaan, so that the Israelites could see for themselves how plentiful it was.

You will need

No equipment is needed.

How to play

Split the children into teams of between four and eight players. You will need at least two teams. Ask each team to select a 'bringer' (this person can be changed during the game to give other children a chance).

Explain that you are going to ask the children to bring you various items and that the first bringer to place that item in your hand will get a point. Make it clear that only the bringer can give you the item: if any other child runs to you, it will not be counted. Point out that any item you ask for must not be attached to someone's body. For example, if you ask for a shoe, it must be taken off someone's foot before it is brought to you. Examples of what you might say include:

- Bring me a sock
- Bring me a hair band
- Bring me a Bible

- Bring me a hat
- Bring me a watch
- Bring me a coat
- Bring me a hair bobble
- Bring me a leader
- Bring me a tissue

Helpful hint

At least initially, ask for items that the children are likely to have easy access to.

*

JOSHUA: RAHAB AND JERICHO

Story reference: Joshua 1—2

Collect the rope

Age banding
4–7 (Reception to Year 3)
All ages

Aim
To remind the children that God kept his promise to keep Rahab and everyone in her household safe.

You will need

Ideally, red wool, but paper and some imagination will do fine. Quickly cut the paper into thin strips of different lengths. If wool is available, cut different lengths.

How to play
Spread the pieces of red wool around the room. Split the children into even teams and explain that they have to collect one piece of wool at a time and take it to a team leader. Once they have handed one piece of wool to the leader, they can then go to find another piece, and so on.

The leader will place the pieces of wool on the floor to make a long line (Rahab's rope). When all the pieces of wool have been collected, the lines are measured. The winning team is the one with the longest 'rope'.

A variation of this game is to request that the children themselves form a 'rope' as they move round collecting the wool. Ask the children to hold on to each other's hands, with the first child leading the way and the last child in the rope picking up the piece of wool. Once the wool has been delivered to the leader, the first child moves to the back of the line so that a different child then leads the rope forward.

Helpful hints

- If wool is available, the ropes can be tied together by an adult leader.
- You may like to do this as a timed activity to add a bit more excitement.

Find the spy!

Age banding
7–11 (Years 3 to 6)
All ages

Aim
To remind the children that Rahab hid the spies on her roof.

You will need

Nine chairs; pieces of paper with a, b, c and 1, 2, 3 written on them (optional)

How to play

Place the nine chairs in a square formation. Place the letters on the floor in front of the chairs and the numbers up the side of the chairs to act as coordinates, if required.

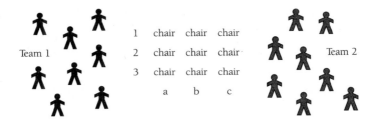

	a	b	c
1	chair	chair	chair
2	chair	chair	chair
3	chair	chair	chair

Ask the children to imagine that this is Rahab's roof. You are going to secretly write down which chair the spy is sitting on—for example, a2 or c1 and so on.

Split the children into two teams, with at least five players in each team. Ask nine of the children to sit on the chairs (four from one team and five from the other). Now ask the remaining team members to take turns at guessing which chair the 'spy' is sitting on. If an incorrect chair is chosen, the child sitting on that chair moves to join the rest of their team. Someone else then makes a guess. When the spy is found, the team that guessed the coordinate correctly receives five points. It makes no difference which team the spy is on.

Once the spy has been found, the game restarts with a different secret coordinate written down by a leader and different children on the chairs. Alternate the teams so that they take turns in having four children or five children on the chairs.

Helpful hints

- With younger children, ask them to point to the chair they think the spy is sitting on, as they probably won't understand coordinates.
- If there are lots of children, use 16 chairs rather than nine.

1	chair	chair	chair	chair
2	chair	chair	chair	chair
3	chair	chair	chair	chair
4	chair	chair	chair	chair
	a	b	c	d

*

GIDEON

Story reference: Judges 6—7

Mighty warrior!

Age banding
4–7 (Reception to Year 3)
All ages

Aim
To remind the children that God called Gideon a 'mighty warrior'.

You will need
Something to mark out a 'home' area, such as a rope, tape, chairs and so on; something to mark where Gideon stands, such as a mat, rope, hoop and so on.

How to play
At one end of the room, mark a small area in which one child, 'Gideon', will stand. At the opposite end of the room, mark out a 'home' area.

Home

Ask one child to pretend to be Gideon and stand at one end of the room. Ask all the other children to stand in the opposite 'home' area. When you indicate the start of the game, all the children walk towards Gideon and then around him or her while they say the rhyme:

'Mighty warrior,' God did say.
Catch us or we'll run away!

Gideon simply stands still and then suddenly, without warning, he or she leaps up in the air and tries to tag as many children as possible before they reach 'home'. The child that was tagged first becomes Gideon and the game continues.

Helpful hint

This is an easy game once the children have got the hang of it. However, it is often easier if a leader is the first person to be Gideon, to demonstrate. The game can be played simply for fun or the children who get tagged can be called 'out' and the game repeated until only one person escapes home. This child is the winner and becomes Gideon.

Catch the Midianite

Age banding
7–11 (Years 3 to 6)

Aim
To remind the children that when the Midianites fled from Gideon and his army, some of them were caught and some escaped.

You will need

No equipment is needed.

How to play

Ask all the children, apart from two, to stand in a circle. Explain that one of the children outside the circle is an escaping Midianite and the other child is Gideon or one of the Israelite soldiers. Ask the children in the circle to join hands and spread out so that there are gaps between them but they can still comfortably hold each other's hands in the air.

The Midianite has three seconds to escape before the Israelite sets off to catch him or her. The children in the circle count to three. The Midianite can weave in and out of the circle as he or she chooses—straight across, or in and out, going under the arms of the children in the circle. The Israelite must follow the exact path that the Midianite takes. If the Midianite is caught, the Israelite becomes the Midianite and a new Israelite is selected from the circle. If the Midianite is not caught, you may want to swap the Israelite after a while, for a fresher pair of legs!

Helpful hint

If the game seems too easy, allow the 'circle' to act as obstacles. For example, they could lift their arms for the Midianite but move their arms up and down when the Israelite wants to pass.

＊

SAMSON

Story reference: Judges 13—16

Where are the Philistines?

Age banding
4–7 (Reception to Year 3)

Aim
To remind the children that Samson's enemies were the Philistines.

You will need
A blindfold, such as a scarf, or hat pulled over the children's eyes. (Alternatively, trust the children to keep their eyes shut.)

How to play
Select one child to be Samson. This child stands, blindfolded, in the centre of the room with all the other children standing round the outer edge of the room. In a loud voice Samson calls, 'Where are the Philistines?' Samson continues to call this as many times as he wants. All the other children try to sneak forward without making a noise and gently touch Samson before darting away. At the same time Samson tries to catch any 'Philistine' he thinks is near him.

Once the 'Philistines' have touched Samson and escaped, they must return to touch the wall before attempting to touch him again. The game continues with the children creeping forward until Samson catches one of them. This child then takes on the role of Samson.

Helpful hint

This game can be played to reinforce many Bible stories where someone is captured in some way. For example, for Jonah and the whale, Jonah stands in the circle and shouts, 'Where is the whale?' For Saul and David, Saul stands in the circle and shouts, 'Where is David?'

In the dark

Age banding
7–11 (Years 3 to 6)
All ages

Aim
To emphasise how difficult it would have been for Samson to be blind.

You will need

Blindfolds, such as scarves, pieces of cloth, kitchen roll or jumpers; chairs.

How to play
Set the chairs out in a random pattern around the room. Place the children in teams. Explain that one person in each team will be blindfolded while the rest of their team will shout instructions to

tell them how to make their way through the chairs to the other side of the room. Place the blindfolded children at their starting places and start the race.

The children are likely to be noisy! When the teams have competed with all the children shouting directions, blindfold a different child in each team, but this time ask just one team member of each team to give directions. Point out that noises coming from different directions can be very confusing for blind people.

Helpful hint

Alter the course for each 'race', as the children will quickly remember which way to go.

---

*

RUTH

Story reference: The book of Ruth

Cold feet!

Age banding
4–7 (Reception to Year 3)

Aim
To remind the children of the visit that Ruth made to Boaz.

You will need

Something to cover a child's feet, such as a coat or towel.

How to play
Sit all the children in a circle on the floor. Select one child to sit in the middle of the circle with their legs stretched out. Place the cover over their feet: they are 'Boaz'. Boaz must keep his or her eyes closed and head down. (Use a blindfold if necessary.)

When everyone is ready, point to one child in the circle. This child must then creep to the centre of the circle and steal the cloth from Boaz's feet. If Boaz hears a sound, he or she must point in the direction of the sound. If Boaz points directly at the 'creeper', they must return to their place. Another child is then selected to have a turn at creeping. If the cloth is removed successfully from Boaz's feet, the creeper takes the place of Boaz.

Helpful hint

This game can be played to reinforce many Bible stories by changing the item that is placed near the person in the centre—for example, Rebekah in the centre with a pot in front of her, representing her water jug; Joseph in the centre with a multi-coloured coat; Noah with a cuddly animal from the ark, and so on.

You're welcome

Age banding

7–11 (Years 3 to 6)
All ages

Aim

To help the children realise that, just as Boaz welcomed Ruth who was a newcomer to his town, we too need to talk to new people.

You will need

Music CD and CD player (optional).

How to play

Split the children into two equal groups and ask them to stand in two concentric circles, facing each other. Each child should be opposite a partner. Ask the children to carry out an action with their partner, such as 'Shake hands five times'.

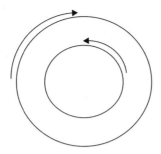

Explain that when you shout 'Go', you want the children to walk round in their circles in opposite directions until you shout 'Stop!' Alternatively, play music and ask the children to move round in their circles until the music stops. When the children stop, they should be opposite different partners.

Give the children an instruction, such as 'Join hands and spin five times'. Then shout 'Go' again or play the music. Each time the circles stop, a different action is given, which each child must carry out with the child opposite them.

Suggestions for actions could include:

- Hum a song that your partner has to guess
- Pull a scary face
- Shake hands four times with each hand and then four times with both
- Find out your partner's hobbies
- Find out your partner's favourite food

Helpful hint

Keep track of which children have been partnered with each other and try to make sure the children stop opposite a lot of different partners.

*

SAUL

Story reference: 1 Samuel 16:14–23; 9:1—10:1

Whose is the instrument?

Age banding
4–7 (Reception to Year 3)

Aim
To help the children remember that when King Saul felt unwell, he would send for David to play his harp.

You will need
No equipment is needed.

How to play
Show the children an action for plucking a harp and ask them to copy the action. Now explain that you want each of them to think of a different musical instrument and make up an action to show how that instrument would be played. Point out that the children are not to make any noises. Give everyone a short time to think about or discuss different instruments, and then go round the group asking each child to show their action. Make sure everyone has a different instrument.

Now select one child to be the conductor. The conductor begins by 'playing' his or her own instrument and all the other children copy what he or she is doing. After a short time, the conductor suddenly swaps to perform the action of one of the other children and, as he swaps, he says the name of that child. The named child now becomes the conductor. She plays her instrument for a short while before swapping to a different child's action and saying that child's name.

For example, Daniel is the conductor and starts playing the guitar. Daniel changes to play the drums and says Richard's name. (Richard had originally been playing drums.) Richard is now the conductor. He plays the drums for a while, then starts to play the flute while saying Ruth's name. (Ruth was originally playing the flute.) Ruth is now the conductor, and so it goes on.

Helpful hint

A simpler version of this game is to have the children taking it in turns to conduct the orchestra. One child is selected as the conductor and keeps swapping from one instrument to another while the other children copy them. After a while, a different conductor is chosen and the orchestra follows his or her lead.

Moving the donkeys

Age banding
7–11 (Years 3 to 6)
All ages

Aim
To help the children remember the story of Saul's search for his father's donkeys.

You will need

Two pieces of card for each team, in different colours if possible; paper cut or torn into shapes approximately 8cm x 8cm (to represent the 'donkeys').

How to play

Split the children into teams of between six and ten and ask them to stand in lines, one behind the other. Place two pieces of card on the floor beside the first person in each line. On one of these pieces of card, place a pile of 20 'donkeys'.

On your signal, the first child picks up a donkey and hands it to the second in line, who passes it on to the next child and so on. As soon as the second child has taken the first donkey, the first child picks up the next donkey and passes that on. He or she then picks up the third donkey and passes that on. This is continued until all the donkeys in the pile have been passed down the line.

When the first donkey reaches the end of the line, it must be passed back along the line but this time behind people's backs. Donkeys will therefore be passing up and down the line in opposite directions, and in front of and behind people. When the first child in the line receives a donkey back, they place it on the second piece of card on the floor. The first team to return all their donkeys is the winner.

Helpful hints

- Check that the children pass the donkeys separately, not in piles. For smaller numbers, time how long it takes for all the donkeys to make the journey. Then challenge the children to try to complete the task in a quicker time.
- Donkeys can be represented by anything small, such as drinking straws, screwed-up bits of paper, paper-clips and so on. If the game is prepared beforehand, pictures of donkeys would be great!

*

SAMUEL

Story reference: 1 Samuel 3

'Samuel, Samuel'

Age banding
4–7 (Reception to Year 3)
All ages

Aim
To remind the children that, when Samuel first heard God's voice, he didn't recognise it.

You will need
A chair.

How to play
Ask all the children to sit in a group on the floor, and place a chair a short distance away from them. Select one child to sit on the chair with their back towards the rest of the children. This person is 'Samuel'.

Explain that when Samuel is not looking, you will select one of the children in the group. They must say 'Samuel, Samuel' in a funny voice and the person on the chair has to try to guess who is speaking. If Samuel guesses incorrectly, the speaker continues to repeat 'Samuel, Samuel' in a funny voice until he or she is guessed correctly. At this point, another Samuel is chosen to sit on the chair and a different speaker is secretly selected.

Helpful hint

This is a good game for leaders to join in. Children love to hear their leaders speaking in silly voices.

Listening twist

Age banding

7–11 (Years 3 to 6)

Aim

To remind the children that Samuel needed to listen to what God said.

You will need

No equipment is needed.

How to play

Split the children into teams of about six and ask them to stand in a circle and number themselves 1 to 6.

Explain to the children that you are going to read out some instructions that you want them to follow, even if they get in a muddle. The children should hold their position while other children carry out their instructions.

Instructions
- Number 3 place your left hand on number 5's right foot.
- Number 1 place your right hand on number 6's right elbow.
- Number 4 place your left knee against number 2's left knee.

- Number 5 place your right hand on number 4's head.
- Number 4 place your left knee against number 1's right knee.
- Number 2 place your left hand on number 3's shoulder.
- Number 6 place your left hand on number 2's head.
- Number 3 place your right knee on number 5's elbow.
- Number 1 place your left foot on number 4's right foot.
- Number 2 place your right hand on number 3's head.
- Number 6 place your left elbow against number 1's right elbow.
- Number 5 place your left hand on number 6's knee.

Carry on giving instructions of this kind. The game can be simply played for fun or the last team to not fall over can be declared the winner.

Helpful hint

Place a leader with each team to check that the children don't get too silly.

*

DAVID AND GOLIATH

Story reference: 1 Samuel 17

David's aim!

Age banding
4–7 (Reception to Year 3)
All ages

Aim
To remind the children that, when David defeated Goliath, it was not an easy task.

You will need

A target, such as an empty plastic bottle or a book standing on its bottom edge (use more targets for larger groups); something to throw, such as screwed-up balls of paper; a scary face, drawn quickly on to a piece of paper and attached to the target to make the game more realistic (optional).

How to play
Ask the children to stand in a line behind a chair. Place the target at a sensible distance from the children. Explain that they are going to take it in turns to throw the 'ball' at the target, aiming to hit it or knock it over. The children could be given a point each time they hit the target if an overall winner is required, or they could just play for fun. Move the target further away as the children's aim improves.

Victory!

Age banding

7–11 (Years 3 to 6)

Aim

To remind the children that, because of David's actions, the Israelites won the war against the Philistines.

You will need

Paper torn into small pieces; a hat or bowl (optional); chairs.

How to play

Ask the children to sit on chairs in a circle, facing inwards. Tear the paper into as many pieces as there are players. On one piece of paper draw an 'X', but leave all the other pieces blank. Fold up the pieces of paper and place them in a container, such as a hat or bowl, or hold them in your cupped hands. Ask each child to take a piece of paper, secretly open it, look at it and fold it up again. When everyone has looked, collect the papers, ready for the next game.

Explain that only one person had an 'X' on their paper, and he or she is 'David'. The rest of the children are Philistines and, one by one, David is going to get rid of them until he has won the battle. David will do this by secretly winking at other children one by one. He or she must try to do this without anyone else spotting the wink. If a child is winked at, that child must get up from his or her chair and stand behind it. They must not say who winked at them and they are not allowed to make a guess or give clues to the other children.

David's aim is to get all the children to stand behind their chairs before anyone guesses correctly who David is. If someone thinks they know who David is, they may put up their hand and take a guess. If they are correct, the game is over and a new game begins. If the guess is incorrect, the guesser moves to stand behind their chair and the game continues.

Helpful hint

Make sure the children can't see through the paper you use, or else everyone will know who David is before he or she starts winking!

*

DAVID, SAUL AND JONATHAN

Story reference: 1 Samuel 20

'Saul, Saul... David'

Age banding
4–7 (Reception to Year 3)

Aim
To remind the children that Jonathan sneaked around trying to find out Saul's plan for David, and then secretly saved him.

You will need
No equipment is needed.

How to play
Ask all the children to sit in a circle with room on the outside to run round. Choose one child to be Jonathan. Jonathan walks round the outside of the circle and, as he passes each child, he gently touches the person's head and says, 'Saul... Saul... Saul... David.' Jonathan may say 'Saul' as many or as few times as he likes.

If, when Jonathan touches a child's head, he or she says 'Saul', nothing happens. If, when Jonathan touches a child's head, he or she says 'David', the child who is touched jumps up and chases Jonathan round the circle.

If David catches Jonathan, then Jonathan is still on. If Jonathan gets back to David's place before he or she is caught, David becomes Jonathan.

Helpful hint

This game can be played to reinforce any Bible story by renaming the characters. For example, use 'Jonah', 'Nineveh', 'whale'; names of prophets; Shadrach, Meshach, Abednego, and so on.

1, 2, 3, fire!

Age banding
7–11 (Years 3 to 6)
All ages

Aim
To remind the children of Jonathan's skill with a bow and arrow, which led to David's escape.

You will need

A target, such as a chair, a box, a plastic bottle or similar; a book or several books; screwed-up pieces of paper about the size of tennis balls; some masking tape or chalk (optional).

How to play
Mark a line on the floor and ask all the children to stand behind it. (Standing behind a chair is fine.) Place the target at a sensible

distance from the children and ask them to imagine that it is the pile of stones that Jonathan aimed for. Hold a book in front of you, with its cover facing your chest and with your hands positioned at the bottom. Position your fingers in front and your thumbs behind the book. Bend your hands backwards.

Place a ball of paper at the top end of the book. Show the children that, if you now flip your hands, you will be able to 'fire' the ball in the air. The aim is to hit the pile of stones. If there are lots of children, set up more targets. Encourage the children to realise how skilful Jonathan was.

Helpful hint

If the children hit the target too easily, move the target further away or make it smaller. Set up a few targets of varying difficulty so that every child has the chance of achieving their aim.

*

SOLOMON

Story reference: 1 Kings 3; 4:29–34

Solomon's memory

Age banding
4–7 (Reception to Year 3)
All ages

Aim
To remind the children that, as well as being very wise, Solomon also committed to memory lots of information about plants, animals, insects and fish.

You will need

A selection of 20 objects collected quickly from around the room, such as scissors, hair bobble, pen, rubber, Bible, piece of paper, scarf, cup, spoon, ring, drawing-pin and so on; a cover such as a coat, jumper, tablecloth or similar.

How to play
Place the objects on to a table, one at a time, until all 20 are there. Explain that the children have one minute to look at the objects, after which you are going to cover them up. You want them to remember as many of the objects as they can without looking.

If there are enough children, this game works well with the children divided into two teams. A leader or older child then writes down all the objects that the team can remember. If there are just a few children, ask the children to put up their hands and tell you one object at a time. Write each object on a piece of paper as the children name it.

When the children can't think of any more objects, remove the cover and see what they have forgotten.

Helpful hint

Children enjoy a variation of this game where they are allowed to collect 20 objects and place them on a table for you to memorise!

Answering wisely

Age banding

7–11 (Years 3 to 6)

Aim

To remind the children that Solomon showed great wisdom when he answered the questions that people asked.

You will need

No equipment is needed.

How to play

Ask for one volunteer who thinks they could be good at answering questions. Ask this child to come to the front. Explain that you are going to ask them lots of questions. They can answer in any way they want, but they must not say 'Yes' or 'No'. Point out that nodding or shaking their head is not allowed: they must actually speak.

Questions could include:

- Is your name Ben? (Child answers 'It is.')
- Do you go to school? ('I do.')
- How old are you? ('Nine.')
- Did you say 9? ('That's what I said.')
- Do you like school? ('It's OK.')
- What do you like best at school? ('Maths.')
- Maths!? ('Yes'—child has been caught out!)

The idea is that you want to trip the child up, so questions need to be asked quickly one after another. Once the first child is out, invite another volunteer to the front. The game can continue in this way or the children can split into small groups and a few children can have a go at catching out one of their own group.

Helpful hint

Children enjoy trying to catch out their leaders. However, don't try to stay in for the whole session (even if you could!) as the children will want to have a go themselves.

---

*

JEROBOAM AND REHOBOAM

Story reference: 1 Kings 11:26—12:25

Jigsaw relay

Age banding
4–7 (Reception to Year 3)

Aim
To remind the children that the prophet Ahijah tore his cloak into twelve pieces to demonstrate how the Israelites would be split apart.

You will need
Two paper coat shapes cut out of A4 paper (see template below); four chairs (optional).

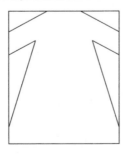

How to play

Show the children the two paper coats. Explain that, just like Ahijah, you are going to divide each coat into twelve pieces. With them watching, cut each coat into twelve pieces and place them in separate piles.

Divide the children into two teams and ask them to line up behind a chair. Place two other chairs a short distance away from each team, with the jigsaw pieces piled on top of them. Alternatively, place the pieces on the floor.

ᚠᚠᚠᚠᚠᚠ   chair   chair

chairs with pieces on

ᚠᚠᚠᚠᚠᚠ   chair   chair

On your instruction, the first child in each team runs to collect one piece of their jigsaw and take it back to their team. The second child then runs to collect a second piece, and so on. The rest of the team can be putting together the jigsaw as the children run to collect further pieces. The winners are the first team to be sitting in a line with their jigsaw completed correctly.

Helpful hint

To make the game easier, place the completed jigsaw on the chair so that the children simply have to collect the pieces and place them near their team in the correct formation.

The biggest coat

Age banding
7–11 (Years 3 to 6)
All ages

Aim
To help the children understand that, after Solomon's reign, the Israelites were split into two groups: Israel (ten northern tribes) and Judah. The prophet Ahijah showed this pictorially by tearing his cloak.

You will need

Two coats of different sizes (jumpers or sweatshirts and your imagination will do).

How to play
Divide the children into two equal teams of an odd number, such as 5, 7, 9 or 11, and ask them to line up behind a starting point. Place the two coats at the other end of the room (one coat must be big and one small). On your signal, the first person in each team runs to the coats. Whoever gets there first takes the bigger coat; the second person takes the smaller coat.

Each child takes the coat back to the second person in their own line. The second person runs to put the coat back at the opposite end of the room, then runs to the third person and touches their hand. The third person runs to get a coat, and so on. (The odd numbers collect the coat and the even numbers put it back.)

The aim of the game is to be the team that has possession of the larger coat when everyone has run. This isn't just a speed race; it is a game of skill. The children can use tactics such as slowing down to make sure their team gets the large coat, especially towards the end of the game.

Helpful hint

If there are more than two teams, you will need more coats (the same number of coats as there are teams). It is important that one coat is visibly bigger than the others, however, as that is the one which will win the game.

*

ELIJAH

Story reference: 1 Kings 17—18

Making rain

Age banding
4–7 (Reception to Year 3)

Aim
To remind the children that Elijah gave the prophecy that there would be no rain on the land.

You will need
No equipment is needed.

How to play
For this game the children need to be taught a series of actions.

1. Rubbing their palms together as quickly as they can.
2. Patting their knees or thighs with the flat part of their hands.
3. Stamping their feet on the floor (quietly and then more noisily).
4. Clapping their fingers together (this makes slightly less noise than clapping together their whole hands).

The idea is that the children follow your lead to make the rainfall sound different. You may set off by clapping your fingers quietly together, then increase the speed and put in the occasional foot stamp. You may then have a torrential downpour with feet stamping and knees patted, followed by hands being rubbed together. The actions may then calm down to create a steady rainfall until the rain eventually stops.

If the children struggle to follow your lead, say words to make it clear what you are doing—for example, rub, pat, stamp, clap. When the children have mastered the instructions, add extra features, such as suddenly shouting 'Sunshine!' at which point the children have to jump up, put their hands in the air and wiggle their fingers as if they were the sun's rays. Other commands could include the following:

- 'Snow': the children wrap their arms around themselves as if they are shivering, and make their teeth chatter.
- 'Hailstone': the children curl up on the floor in a small ball (as if they are a hailstone).

Helpful hint

Once the children have got the hang of this game, choose a child to be the leader so that the other children follow his or her lead rather than yours. Allow several children to take a turn at being the leader. The children will especially love it if you join in as well.

Follow the brook

Age banding

7–11 (Years 3 to 6)
All ages

Aim

To remind the children that, during the drought, Elijah was directed by God to go to Cherith Brook, where he would find water and also be provided with food.

You will need

No equipment is needed.

How to play

Ask for a volunteer to come to the front. (You may like to ask for a child who is not too ticklish!) Ask the child to roll up one of their sleeves or take off their jumper so that the whole of his or her forearm can be seen. Explain that you want the children to imagine that your finger is Elijah walking to find Cherith Brook (the place of safety to which God directed him). The crease made by the elbow bending is Cherith Brook. Explain that you are slowly going to make Elijah 'walk' along the path (arm) to Cherith Brook (crease). You want the volunteer to look away and guess when you arrive at the brook.

Now, with the volunteer looking away (check they don't cheat!), slowly move your finger from side to side along his or her arm, moving slowly towards the crease. Keep reminding the volunteer that they must say 'now' when they think you have 'arrived' (reached the crease). You will be surprised at the answer!

Demonstrate on another child and see if they can be more

accurate. Now let the children have a go on each other. Let them swap to have a go on other friends.

Helpful hint

This works best if you don't touch the crease in the volunteer's arm before you start; simply point to it without making contact. The activity also works best if your movements are slow as you 'tickle' the arm.

---

*

ELISHA

Story reference: 2 Kings 4:8–37; 5:1–19

Find a room

Age banding
4–7 (Reception to Year 3)
All ages

Aim
To remind the children that the woman from Shunem made a special room for Elisha on the roof of her home.

How to play
Ask one child to be Elisha and then split the remaining children into groups of three. Ask two of the children in each group to face each other and join their hands to represent a room. Ask the third child to stand in the centre of the room.

Explain that Elisha wants to find a room to stay in but, at the moment, all the rooms are full. Elisha will therefore walk round and suddenly clap his or her hands or shout 'change'. At this point, all the children standing in a room have to move to a different room and Elisha has to find a room to move into. If Elisha succeeds, a different child will now be left without a room. This child now becomes Elisha and walks round until he or she decides to clap (or shout 'change'), at which point all the children swap rooms again.

Continue playing the game until a number of children have had a turn at being Elisha.

Helpful hints

You may like to demonstrate the game with a leader playing the part of Elisha. This game can be played to accompany many Bible stories. For example:

- Paul in prison (the children pretend they are prisons rather than rooms and the child outside shouts 'Escape!')
- Jonah (the children are 'big fish' rather than rooms and the child outside shouts 'Save me!')
- Zacchaeus (the children are trees rather than rooms and the child outside shouts 'Hurry down!')

'I spot'

Age banding
7–11 (Years 3 to 6)

Aim
To remind the children that Naaman had leprosy before the prophet Elisha told him to wash in the River Jordan and he was healed.

You will need

Something to use as spots, such as squares of paper, stickers or sticky notes. Alternatively, give each child a piece of paper to hold, on to which you can draw spots in pen.

How to play

Ask the children to sit in a circle facing each other. (If you are using paper and pen to record the game, give each child a blank piece of paper to hold. This paper must be held so that all the other children can see it.) Explain that the children need to learn a few words before the game begins. One child says 'I, (insert own name), have no spots. How many spots have you, (insert someone else's name)?' The second child repeats the words above, adding another child's name instead of their own.

For example, 'I, Charis, have no spots. How many spots have you, Laura?' 'I, Laura, have no spots. How many spots have you, Harriet?' 'I, Harriet, have no spots. How many spots have you, Oliver?' 'I, Oliver, have no spots. How many spots have you, Reanne?'

Once the children have had a practice, explain that if they are too slow, get their words wrong or say the words directly back to the child who just picked them, they will be given a spot. This spot can be a sticker or a mark drawn on their paper, but it must be visible to the other children. If a child has a spot, they must remember and, when it is their turn to speak, say, 'I, Laura, have one spot. How many spots have you, Oliver?' If they have two spots, they say, 'I, Oliver, have two spots. How many spots have you, Lydia?'

If a child forgets they have spots and says 'no spots' (or says the wrong number of spots), they receive another spot. The aim of the game is to get as few spots as possible.

Helpful hint

As the children pick up the words, you can become stricter about mistakes. The game is more fun if more spots are given.

*

THE TIME OF THE KINGS

Story reference: Various

May I come closer?

Age banding
4–7 (Reception to Year 3)
All ages

Aim
To remind the children that, in the Old Testament, the kings were very powerful and ordinary people needed special permission to come into their presence.

You will need
No equipment is needed.

How to play
Ask all the children to stand at one end of the room. Choose one child to be the king. The king needs to stand as far away as possible from the other children and must face away from them. He or she must not turn round at all during the game.

king

Explain that, when you point to a child, they must say to the king in a funny voice, 'May I come closer, king?' The king will always answer 'Yes' but must also say whether the child can take large or small steps and how many steps they can take.

For example, you point to Rose. Rose asks, 'May I come closer, king?' The king says, 'Yes. Take three big steps.' Rose obeys the king. You point to Josh. Josh now asks, 'May I come closer, king?' The king says, 'Yes. Take four little steps.' Josh obeys the king.

The game ends when any child gets close enough to touch the king. At this point, a different king is chosen and the game is repeated.

Helpful hints

- The children will need to disguise their voices and may need to talk more loudly or quietly to disguise whether or not they are near the king.
- Once the children are used to the easy version of the game, the rules can be made more complicated. For example, rather than just large and small steps, you may introduce leaps or giant steps, or even 'one step forward and two steps back'.

Kingdoms!

Age banding

7–11 (Years 3 to 6)

Aim

To remind the children that, in Old Testament times, many areas were governed by kings who fought against other countries in the hope of extending their own kingdoms. God granted the Israelites their wish to be governed by their own king. The Bible states that some of these kings followed God, while others didn't.

You will need

A piece of paper and a pen.

How to play

Ask the children to sit on chairs in a circle. Ask them all to think of a famous character whose name they are going to use for their 'kingdom'. The character may be a famous person from the past such as Winston Churchill, a cartoon character such as Mickey Mouse, a sportsperson such as David Beckham, or any character that the other children will have heard of.

Ask each child to come to you in turn and secretly tell you the character they have chosen. (Make sure the other children can't hear.) Write all the names of the characters on a piece of paper. (Don't list the characters in order, or some children will work out which children have selected which character.) Now add one extra character to the list as a red herring. You should now have a list that has one more character on it than the number of children.

Read the list of names out to the children, making sure that no one acknowledges who they are. Select one child to start the game. This child asks another child, 'Are you (for example) Winston Churchill?' If the child says 'No', it is their turn to ask a different child.

For example, Angela starts by asking, 'Kelly, are you Winston Churchill?' Kelly replies, 'No... James, are you Donald Duck?' James answers, 'No... Skye, are you Darcy Bussell?' Skye says, 'No... Ben, are you Thomas the Tank Engine?' Ben says, 'Yes!'

When a child is guessed correctly, that child moves to sit at the feet of the person who made the correct guess. So, in the example above, Ben would go to sit at Skye's feet. Ben now becomes part of Skye's kingdom; they can work together to work out the other characters. Skye now has another turn. If she again guesses another child correctly, that child also moves to sit at her feet. If Skye guesses incorrectly, the game continues as above.

You will need to keep reading the list of characters out to the children so that they can remember who is on the list. As characters are guessed correctly, cross the names off your list so that fewer names are read out. Eventually there will be two children left who, between them, have all the other children sitting at their feet. At this point there should be three names on your list, one of which is your red herring. Whichever child guesses the other's character first will therefore 'win' all the other 'kingdoms'. They are the ultimate victor and have won the game.

Helpful hints

- You may want to write the list of characters on a large piece of paper so that the children can keep referring to it.
- This game gets better each time you play it, as children work out special strategies for staying in the game longer—usually by choosing characters that no one would normally associate with them. The first time you play, children will pick their favourite cartoon character or favourite pop star, enabling their friends to guess easily who they are.

✳

NEHEMIAH

Story reference: The book of Nehemiah

Funny faces!

Age banding
4–7 (Reception to Year 3)
All ages

Aim
To remind the children that King Artaxerxes noticed that Nehemiah looked sad.

You will need
No equipment is needed.

How to play
Ask the children to sit in a circle facing each other. Explain that you are going to choose one child to start the game. The child has to walk over to someone, say their name and then pull a face showing a particular expression, such as sad, smiley, funny and so on. The child who was named has to pull the same face back and then stand up so that the first child can take their seat. This child then walks over to someone else, says that person's name and pulls a different face. The aim of the game is to keep from laughing. The game can be played just for fun or children can be called 'out' if they laugh.

Helpful hint

This game works best if leaders join in. Children often like to see them being silly. For larger groups, have two children pulling the faces at once.

I pass these swords crossed

Age banding
7–11 (Years 3 to 6)

Aim
To remind the children that Nehemiah and his men had to work while holding their weapons, in case their enemies attacked them.

You will need

Two sheets of A4 paper rolled into thin tubes, or two pencils or pens.

How to play
Before you begin, make sure one or two leaders know the secret behind this game.

Ask the children to sit in a circle. Explain that you have two swords (rolls of paper or pencils) and you are going to pass them to the child on your right. That child will then pass them to the child on their right, and so on, until the swords have passed all the way round the circle.

As the swords are passed, each child must say either 'I pass these swords crossed' or 'I pass these swords uncrossed.' You will tell each child if they have said the correct words. The aim of the game is for the children to work out how they can be certain that the words they say are correct every time.

The key is that if, when the child passes on the swords, the leader's legs are crossed over each other in any way (even crossed feet count), the words must be, 'I pass these swords crossed.' However, if their legs are not crossed in any way, the words will be, 'I pass these swords uncrossed.' The children will be so busy looking at the swords and the way they are held that they will not notice anything about your legs.

Helpful hint

As the game moves on, the leaders who know the secret should make the reason for the words slightly more obvious, so that the children have some chance of guessing the solution. If the children are still unable to work out the puzzle, the leaders need to make the crossing and uncrossing of their legs very obvious towards the end of the game.

---

*

ESTHER

Story reference: The book of Esther

Queenie-O, Queenie-O

Age banding
4–7 (Reception to Year 3)
All ages

Aim
To remind the children that Queen Esther risked her life when she went before the king. She knew that if he held out his sceptre she was safe.

How to play
Select one child to be Queen Esther. Ask Esther to stand at one side of the room, with all the other children in a line some distance away from her. The distance can be varied according to the room available. Give Esther the sceptre and ask her to turn her back on the other children.

Esther

On your signal, Esther throws the sceptre over her head into the space between her and the other children. One of the children collects the sceptre and places it behind their back. This child is now the 'king'. The group of children say together:

'Queenie-O, Queenie-O,
Have you come to see me-O?'

Esther now turns round and guesses which child is holding the sceptre. If Esther guesses incorrectly, she has another guess. If she guesses correctly, then the king (sceptre holder) moves to take Esther's place. The game is now repeated with the new Esther throwing the sceptre over her head.

Helpful hints

- If you have no sticky tape available, simply roll the A4 paper and tuck the ends in to hold the roll in place. If no paper is available, use something else as the sceptre—for example, a sock or bobble hat... and a bit of imagination.
- To make the game easier, you could use a bigger sceptre. You can also vary the difficulty of the game by allowing Esther to ask three children to turn round before she makes her decision about who is holding the sceptre. This makes it more difficult for the kings but easier for Esther.

Grab the sceptre

Age banding

7–11 (Years 3 to 6)

Aim

To remind the children that, when the king held out his sceptre to Queen Esther, it meant that she was safe.

You will need

A container such as a bin, box or similar; a roll of paper (a newspaper rolled up and stuck together with sticky tape is ideal) or a few sheets of A3 paper rolled lengthways and stuck together in a roll; sticky tape; chairs (optional—one less than the number of children).

How to play

Place the chairs in a circle facing inwards, with gaps between them, about an arm's length apart. Place the container in the centre. Place the roll of paper (sceptre) in the container.

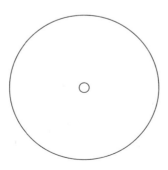

Ask the children to sit on the chairs. Ask one child to stand by the sceptre as if they were the king. Explain that the king will pick up the sceptre and walk round the inside of the circle. Suddenly the king will tap an 'Esther' on the knee with the sceptre. The king immediately runs to place the sceptre back in the bin and then runs out of the circle, passing through one of the gaps by the chair of Esther. At the same time, Esther runs to the centre of the circle and grabs the sceptre from the bin. Esther must then pass out of the circle via one of the gaps by the empty chair.

Esther chases the king round the circle. If the king gets back to the empty chair without being caught, then Esther becomes the king. However, if Esther manages to tap the king with the sceptre before he sits down, the king returns to the centre and has another go.

Helpful hint

Try to ensure that each child gets a turn and that the most popular child doesn't get picked every time. If a leader joins in, they can easily pick children who aren't being chosen and could also let children catch them if they needed some help.

*

ISAIAH

Story reference: The book of Isaiah

Pass the message

Age banding
4–7 (Reception to Year 3)
All ages

Aim
To help the children understand that Isaiah was one of God's prophets. He told the people special messages from God.

You will need

No equipment is needed.

How to play
Ask the children to sit in a line with a gap between them. Make the gaps as big as possible in the space you have available. If there are more than ten children, split them into two teams.

Explain that you are going to whisper a message to the first person in the line. They must then stand up and go to whisper the message to the next person before returning to their original place. The second person then stands up and goes to whisper the message to the next person, and so on. When the message reaches the end of the line, the child says the message out loud. Ask the first child what the original message was: usually the messages are very mixed up.

Suggested messages might include the following:

- Isaiah was a prophet who told the people what God said.
- In the Bible, God spoke to special people called prophets.
- God loves us to do what he asks us.
- Many of the prophets have unusual names.
- Isaiah spoke about God's promised rescuer more than 700 years before Jesus was born.

Helpful hint

Vary the difficulty of the sentence according to the age of the child. This game can be used for any Bible story.

Squeezed message

Age banding

7–11 (Years 3 to 6)

Aim

To help the children see that God gave messages to the prophets. These messages were then passed on to other people.

You will need

One coin; something to grab, such as a beanbag, sock, bobble hat or plastic cup.

How to play

Split the children into two teams and ask them to sit in lines facing each other, about two metres apart. Ask each line to join hands. Position yourself in the middle at one end. Place the object to be grabbed at the other end, within easy reach of the last person in each team.

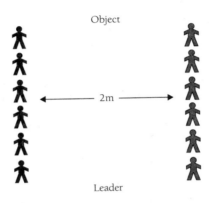

Object

2m

Leader

Explain that you will toss the coin, catch it and hold it on your palm in front of you so that the children sitting nearest you in both teams can see the result at the same time. If the coin shows heads, the first person in each team immediately begins to pass on the message by squeezing the hand of the person next to them. (Make sure the children don't shout out the result of the toss.) This person then squeezes the next person's hand and so on until the message reaches the end of the line nearest the object. As soon as the last person receives the squeeze, they must grab the object before the other team has a chance to do so.

The team that has responded more quickly to the message will have won the game and they receive one point. The person from the winning team who grabbed the object now moves up to the position nearest the leader, to watch the coin being tossed. The rest of the team shuffles down so that there is now a new 'grabber'. The other team stays the same. In this way, children will end up playing against different people.

If the coin lands on tails, then no message should be sent. If, in the excitement, a message is sent by mistake and the object is grabbed, a point is deducted from the team that made the mistake. Team members are not allowed to shout 'Stop!' down the line.

Helpful hint

If you can't find a coin, you could use any object that is small enough to fit in your hand. Place your hands behind your back and, without anyone seeing, place the small object in one hand. Place both closed hands in front of you and then open one hand. If the object is in the hand you opened, the first person in each team should pass the squeeze, as for 'heads' above. If the object is not in your hand, they should not pass the squeeze.

---

*

JEREMIAH

Story reference: Jeremiah 38:1–13

Escape from the well

Age banding
4–7 (Reception to Year 3)
All ages

Aim
To remind the children that Jeremiah was thrown down a well before Ebedmelech rescued him.

You will need

Chairs (one less than the number of players).

How to play
Place the chairs in a circle with a small gap between them. Ask one child to stand in the centre of the circle and ask the other children to sit on the chairs. The central child is 'Jeremiah'. Explain that you are going to make various statements and the children need to listen carefully to what you say. If what you say relates to them, they will need to move out of their chair and swap to another chair. However, Jeremiah will be watching carefully to see if he can escape from the 'well' by sitting on any free chair.

For example, if you say, 'Move if you are wearing blue!' every child wearing anything blue must swap on to another chair. At the same time, Jeremiah will try to sit in a chair that becomes available. The child left without a chair becomes Jeremiah and another statement is made by you. If Jeremiah does not find a free chair, he or she remains in the middle for another go.

Possible statements could include:

- If you are wearing red (or any colour)
- If your name begins with 'M' (or any letter)
- If your birthday is in January (or any month, although younger children may not know)
- If you have a brother or sister
- It you have a bobble in your hair
- If you are wearing trainers
- If you like sausages (or any food)
- If you have brown hair (or any hair colour)
- If you have been in an aeroplane
- If you have been on holiday in a tent

Helpful hint

Try to make sure each child has had an honest reason to move. Most of them will decide to move anyway if they haven't had a go for a few turns.

To the rescue

Age banding

7–11 (Years 3 to 6)

Aim

To remind the children that Ebedmelech led a group of men to rescue Jeremiah when he was thrown down a well.

You will need

A small object such as a coin, peg, key or similar.

How to play

Ask the children to join hands in a circle facing inwards. Ask the children to drop their hands, leaving a small gap between each of them. Ask the children to position their hands so that they are open behind their backs.

Explain that you are going to walk round the circle and discreetly drop a small object into someone's hand. On receiving the object, the child must rush out of the circle (either forwards or backwards) before the two children on either side can catch them. Apart from the child with the object, all the other children must keep their feet in the same position: they cannot chase the escaping child. If the escaping child is caught, they become the one walking round the circle. If the child escapes, they return to the circle and the game continues. The person walking round the circle can pretend to drop the object in children's hands as a decoy.

Helpful hint

If the game proves too difficult and the escaping child is caught every time, make the gaps between the children bigger.

*

DANIEL IN THE LIONS' DEN

Story reference: Daniel 6

Are you sleeping?

Age banding
4–7 (Reception to Year 3)
All ages

Aim
To remind the children that Daniel wasn't harmed when he was thrown in the lions' den, because God closed the mouths of the lions.

You will need

No equipment is needed.

How to play
Ask all the children to lie down on the floor, looking up at the ceiling. They are the lions. Choose one child to be Daniel. Explain that Daniel has to walk round the room, being careful not to stand on the lions. Daniel must lean over one lion and ask, 'Are you sleeping?' He can use a silly voice or pull a funny face at the same time. The lion must reply, 'No, I'm not!' However, the lion cannot open his mouth to speak but must try to say the words without

moving his lips. This usually results in a funny squeaky voice. If the lion says, 'No, I'm not' without laughing, then Daniel moves on to another lion. However, if the lion laughs, he becomes Daniel and Daniel joins the other lions on the floor.

Helpful hint

You may like a leader to be Daniel first, while the children get the hang of the game. The children will also love it if you then join them lying on the floor, pretending to be a lion, especially if you give an occasional roar.

Escape the lion!

Age banding
7–11 (Years 3 to 6)

Aim
To remind the children that Daniel wasn't harmed when he was thrown in the lions' den, because God closed the mouths of the lions.

You will need

Chairs (enough for half the children).

How to play
Place the chairs in a circle facing inwards. Split the children into two equal teams. Ask one team to sit on the chairs in the circle, making sure they leave one chair empty. Ask the other team to position

themselves so that one person is behind each chair, including the empty one. Explain that the children standing are the lions and those seated are trying to get away from them.

The child standing behind the empty chair starts the game by winking at one of the seated children. Immediately the seated child tries to leave his or her chair and dash to the empty one. However, the child standing behind their chair tries to stop them by touching their shoulders. If the child escapes to the empty chair, the lion behind the newly emptied chair takes a turn to wink. If the escaping child is caught, the original lion winks again at a different child.

Helpful hint

After a while, swap the children so that the seated ones become the lions and the standing children sit down.

*

JONAH

Story reference: The book of Jonah

Hidden away

Age banding

4–7 (Reception to Year 3)
All ages

Aim

To remind the children that it is impossible to hide from God.

You will need

A 'Jonah' to hide (a small toy figure that could represent Jonah is ideal, or a small figure cut quickly out of paper).

How to play

Show the children 'Jonah' and explain that they are going to leave the room and you will hide Jonah somewhere in the room. When they return, they will search for Jonah and you will give clues by saying words such as those below. (Make sure the children know what the words mean.)

- **Cold**: a long way from Jonah
- **Hot**: close to Jonah
- **Getting warmer**: moving in the right direction
- **Freezing**: miles away from Jonah

Ask the children to leave the room while you hide Jonah. When the children return and begin to look for Jonah, make comments such as, 'Carmel is freezing but Nathan is warm… Josie almost burnt her hand a moment ago… Becky is getting warmer…' and so on. After a few games, you may want the child who finds Jonah to have a go at hiding the figure and then giving clues.

Helpful hint

If there are lots of children, two or more Jonahs could be hidden in different parts of the room, so that the children don't need to crowd together so much.

Fishes

Age banding
7–11 (Years 3 to 6)

Aim
To remind the children that Jonah was swallowed by a big fish but God rescued him.

You will need

Chairs, one for each child (optional).

How to play
Place the chairs in a circle, facing in a clockwise direction, with a gap between each chair. Ask the children to sit on the chairs. Explain that you are going to give each child the name of a fish

and that you want them to remember which fish they are. Walk round the children and count them off in threes, labelling them (for example) sardine; shrimp; herring. If there are lots of children, use four fish names and count off in fours.

Give the following 'fish' instructions that the children must carry out. (Change the fish names as appropriate.)

- **The herrings went out to sea:** the herrings stand up and start running round the circle.
- **The prawns joined them:** the prawns join the herrings and they run round together.
- **The tide turned:** the 'fish' that are running round change direction and run the opposite way round the circle.
- **There were crocodiles:** the children keep running but snap their hands together at the same time.
- **There were crabs:** the children move round on their hands and feet.
- **There were octopuses:** the children run round waving their arms and legs.
- **There were sea horses:** the children run round galloping like horses.
- **Back to the pond:** the children return to their own place (they need to remember where they sat).
- **Swallowed:** the children have to crouch on the floor. They are not allowed to move, no matter what instruction you give. Even if you shout, 'Back to the pond' they must stay where they are. If you are playing to find a winner, children that do move when an instruction is given are called 'out' and return to their places.
- **Spat out:** the children are released from being 'swallowed' and can stand up and follow instructions again.

When you shout, 'Back to the pond' the children must keep running in the same direction. If you want a winner for this game, the last child back to their place when you say 'back to the pond' is out and turns their chair into the centre. Alternatively, it is good to play so that no one is out and the game is just for fun.

Helpful hint

Don't worry if the children forget what they are. It doesn't really matter if you end up with more shrimps than herrings!

GAMES FOR
NEW TESTAMENT
STORIES

＊

JOHN THE BAPTIST

Story reference: Luke 1:5–25, 39–45, 57–80

What am I?

Age banding
4–7 (Reception to Year 3)
All ages

Aim
To remind the children that Zechariah couldn't speak during the time leading up to the birth of John the Baptist.

You will need
No equipment is needed.

How to play
Explain to the children that, just like Zechariah, they are going to pretend they can't speak. Whisper an action from the list below to one of the children and ask them to act out the action so that the rest of the children can guess what they are doing.

Suggestions for actions might include the following:

- Tying a shoelace
- Riding a bicycle
- Kicking a ball
- Getting dressed

- Opening a packet of crisps
- Making a cake
- Climbing into the car
- Running in a race
- Eating tea
- Making a bed
- Climbing the stairs
- Driving a car

Once the children have had a go at miming the actions, you could move them on to acting out different jobs that people do, from the list below.

- Doctor
- Fire-fighter
- Builder
- Hairdresser
- Teacher
- Post deliverer
- Ballet dancer
- Dentist
- Nurse
- Footballer
- Singer
- Police officer
- Pilot
- Farmer
- Vicar
- Truck driver
- Vet
- Pianist
- Optician
- Athlete

Without words

Age banding

7–11 (Years 3 to 6)

Aim

To remind the children that Zechariah couldn't speak during the time leading up to the birth of John the Baptist.

You will need

The list of words on the next page.

How to play

Split the children into teams of about six. Explain that you have a list of 15 words written down that the children are going to mime to each other in their teams. Explain that one child from each team will come to you and be given a word (the same word for every team). Each child has to go back to their team and, without speaking, mime the word to them. The team has to guess what the word is. When anyone in the team gives an answer, the person miming can nod or shake their head but they must not speak.

Remind the children that if the teams shout out ideas too loudly, the other teams may hear the right answers.

When someone guesses the word being mimed, a different child in the team comes to you, says the word and is given the second word. They then return to their team and mime the second word for the others to guess. The other teams continue with the first word until they come to tell you that word, at which point they are given the second word on the list. The game continues until the end of the list is reached by one team. The first team to complete the list is the winner.

Examples of words might include the following:

ball, lion, fork, ballet dancer, bed, motorbike, necklace, bird, umbrella, pencil, potato peeler, football goal, bath, rollercoaster, giraffe, bus, carrot, wardrobe, tennis racket, newspaper, cricket ball, ice cream, watering can, oak tree, hairdryer, sieve, telephone, doctor, bonfire, window

---

Helpful hints

- If necessary, use the words out of order to give particularly shy or struggling children words that they can mime easily.
- Use the game to reinforce the parts of any Bible story. For example, for the story of the feeding of the 5000, you could use boy, bread, water, lake, hill, basket, fish, grass, children, boat and so on.
- This game is good as an introduction to a lesson, where the game is played and then the children guess which story they are going to hear.

---

*

THE CHRISTMAS STORY

Story reference: Luke 1:26–38; 2:1–20; Matthew 1:18—2:12

Mary's in her house

Age banding
4–7 (Reception to Year 3)

Aim
To remind the children what happened in the Christmas story.

You will need

The tune to the well-known children's rhyme 'The farmer's in his den'.

How to play
Check that the children know the tune to the song 'The farmer's in his den'. Explain that you are going to teach them special Christmas words. The game begins with the children holding hands in a circle, with a child as Mary standing in the centre. As the children sing the words, they walk round, keeping hold of each other's hands.

Verse 1
Mary's in her house
Mary's in her house
An angel came to visit her
Mary's in her house

Mary now chooses someone to be the angel. The angel joins her in the middle of the circle as the second verse is sung.

Verse 2
Mary marries Joe
Mary marries Joe
Then off they go to Bethlehem
Mary marries Joe

The angel chooses a Joseph to join them in the middle.

Verse 3
The baby boy is born
The baby boy is born
The baby's name is Jesus
The baby boy is born

Joseph chooses someone to play the part of the child.

Verse 4
The shepherds come to see
The shepherds come to see
The angel told them they must come
The shepherds come to see

The child chooses a shepherd to join them.

Verse 5
The wise men bring their gifts
The wise men bring their gifts
Frankincense and gold and myrrh
The wise men bring their gifts

The shepherd chooses a wise man to join them in the middle.

Verse Six
We all shout 'hurray'
We all shout 'hurray'
Because it's nearly Christmas
We all shout 'hurray'

As this verse is sung, all the children can swing in toward the middle and shout 'Hurray' loudly together.

Helpful hint

If there are a lot of children, more than one shepherd or wise man can be chosen to stand in the middle.

Noughts and crosses

Age banding
7–11 (Years 3 to 6)
All ages

Aim
To add a twist to a quiz about the Christmas story.

You will need

Nine chairs; a list of questions (see page 132); five pieces of A4 paper with the letter 'O' drawn on them and five pieces with the letter 'X' drawn on them (optional).

How to play

This game is based on 'noughts and crosses', except that the children themselves are the noughts and crosses.

Divide the children into two teams with an equal balance of ages. Work out a way of identifying each team. For example, one team could have their coats on, place their hands on their heads or wear stickers, or all players could hold pieces of paper marked 'O' or 'X'.

Set out nine chairs in a square formation. Ask the two teams to stand on opposite sides of the square and decide which team is to be noughts and which team is to be crosses. It is a good idea to place a marked piece of paper in front of the teams to indicate which symbol will represent each team.

Noughts		Crosses
chair	chair	chair
chair	chair	chair
chair	chair	chair

Explain that you are going to ask each team in turn a question about the Christmas story. If the children know the answer, they must put up their hand. If someone in the first team answers the question correctly, one member of that team positions themselves on the noughts and crosses board by sitting down on a chair. If the first team gets the question wrong, the question swaps to the other team. If this team gives the correct answer, one member of the team positions themselves on the board. It is then the second team's question.

If either team positions their children in a straight line of three, they have won that game. The chairs are emptied and a fresh game begins.

Questions could include the following:

- What was the name of Jesus' mum? (*Mary*)
- How did Mary know she was going to have a baby? (*An angel told her*)
- What was the name of Mary's husband? (*Joseph*)
- What was the name of the town in which Jesus was born? (*Bethlehem*)
- Why did Mary and Joseph travel to Bethlehem? (*To be counted in the census*)
- Which Old Testament prophet spoke about Bethlehem being the place where God's special ruler would be born? (*Micah*)
- What was the baby wrapped in? (*Strips of cloth*)
- Where did Mary place baby Jesus? (*In a manger*)
- Who went to visit Jesus on the night he was born? (*Shepherds*)
- How did the shepherds know Jesus had been born? (*Angels told them*)
- Who did the wise men call to see on the way to find Jesus? (*King Herod*)
- Why was Herod worried? (*He didn't want another king to take his place*)
- What presents did the wise men give to Jesus? (*Gold, frankincense and myrrh: this could count as either one answer or three separate answers*)
- Why did the wise men not return to Herod's palace? (*They were warned about him in a dream*)
- When God warned Joseph in a dream that Herod was looking for Jesus, where did Joseph go with Mary and the baby? (*Egypt*)
- After Herod had died, where did Joseph take Mary and Jesus to live? (*Nazareth*)
- When Jesus was presented at the temple, which elderly woman announced that Jesus was very special? (*Anna*)
- What special promise had God made to Simeon, an elderly man at the temple? (*He would see Jesus before he died*)

Helpful hint

If any children have limited Bible knowledge or younger children are playing, encourage them to be the noughts and crosses so they feel part of things. Make sure you ask the appropriate children the easier questions so that everyone gets a fair go. This is a quick and fun way to revise any Bible story.

*

THE CHRISTMAS STORY

Story reference: Luke 1:26–38; 2:1–20; Matthew 1:18—2:12

This is...

Age banding
4–7 (Reception to Year 3)

Aim
To remind the children about the Christmas story.

You will need

Two empty areas marked out using chairs; the list of Christmas words below.

How to play
Show the children the two areas. Explain that one of the areas is going to show what Christmas is like today and the other is going to show what the first Christmas was like.

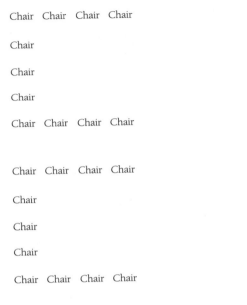

Chair   Chair   Chair   Chair

Chair

Chair

Chair

Chair   Chair   Chair   Chair

Chair   Chair   Chair   Chair

Chair

Chair

Chair

Chair   Chair   Chair   Chair

Ask for a volunteer to act out the first Christmas word for the other children to guess. When the children have correctly guessed the word, ask the children in which area the word would fit. Is it to do with the first Christmas or Christmas today? When the children have decided on the area in which the word would fit, the child who acted the part moves to stand in the area. They are still part of the game and can guess what other children are acting out.

Each child takes it in turns to act out a word and be placed in the correct area. When each child has had a turn, ask the children to repeat their action in the positions they are in. The 'first Christmas' area should have a tableau of the nativity scene built up.

Christmas words include the following (make sure all the characters from the nativity story are used): Christmas tree, donkey, Mary, snowman, angel, star, stocking, Joseph, Christmas lights, shepherd, sheep, sleigh, wise man, manger, cracker, Christmas card, present, camel.

Helpful hint

Some of the children might need help to think of what action to do. The children may also need advice as to where to place themselves in the areas. For example, Mary may want to fetch a chair to sit on, with Joseph standing behind; the shepherds may want to kneel down, and so on.

Christmas pictures

Age banding
7–11 (Years 3 to 6)
All ages

Aim
A fun activity for Christmas!

You will need

Paper and pencils; the list below.

How to play
Split the children into teams of about five and give each team some paper and a pencil. Reassure the children that they don't need to be good at drawing for this game.

Ask one child from each team to come to you. Whisper the first Christmas word from the list to them all. Explain that when you say 'Go', the children will run back to their own team and draw the word they were given. The child is not allowed to speak, make noises or write words. The rest of their team have to try to guess what the word is. When someone guesses the word correctly, that person runs to you. He or she whispers the word to you and is then given the next word on the list. The other teams continue to guess the first word. When they guess it correctly, they come to you to receive the second word.

The same process continues until one team reaches the bottom of the list. It is likely that teams will be on different words most of the time, so it is important that they whisper the word they have just guessed to you so that you know which word they need next.

Use one or two of the lists below for each game.

List 1

- angel
- ribbon
- lights
- manger
- bells
- camel
- field
- Christmas pudding
- book
- wreaths
- decoration
- myrrh

List 2

- present
- tinsel
- bauble
- shepherd
- holly
- star
- Bethlehem
- turkey
- food
- mince pie
- nativity play
- party

List 3

- tree
- stocking
- Advent calendar
- stable
- reindeer
- sheep

- king
- cracker
- chocolate
- sack
- gold
- bows

List 4

- candle
- card
- snowman
- donkey
- snowball
- hill

- dream
- toy
- streamers
- paper
- frankincense
- sweets

Helpful hint

For younger children or those who struggle with drawing, alter the order in which the objects are given so that these children are given easier pictures to draw.

*

THE BOY JESUS IN THE TEMPLE

Story reference: Luke 2:41–52

Line up

Age banding
4–7 (Reception to Year 3)
All ages

Aim
To remind the children that Jesus was once a small boy but he grew up just like we do.

You will need

No equipment is needed.

How to play
Split the children into teams of approximately six. Explain that you are going to ask the children to arrange themselves, depending on different characteristics. The aim of the game is to be the quickest team to follow your instruction correctly.

The instructions are:

- Get into a line in order of height.
- Get into a line in alphabetical order of your names.

- Get into a line in order of age.
- Get into a line in order of the size of your feet.
- Get into a line in order of the month of your birthday (January to December).

After each instruction has been carried out, check that the teams have completed the task correctly. You may like to give points to the winning team in each round and find the overall champion.

Helpful hint

Try to place someone in each team who you know will take some responsibility for organising the group, such as an older child or leader.

Time challenge

Age banding
7–11 (Years 3 to 6)

Aim
To remind the children that Mary and Joseph spent a lot of time searching for Jesus when he went missing.

You will need

A watch or clock with a second hand; paper and pencils.

How to play
As a warm-up for this game, ask the children to stand up. Explain that you want to see if they can guess how long a minute is. (Make

sure all the children know there are 60 seconds in one minute.) Ask them to start counting in their heads when you say 'Go' and to sit down when they think one minute has passed. Make a mental note of the child who sits down closest to one minute and ask them to share their counting technique with the others. Play the game a few times and see if the children can improve on their estimation.

Next, explain to the children that you are going to give them some challenges to see what they can do in one minute. Give each child a piece of paper. Show them a simple drawing of a house. Explain that they are not trying to draw fantastic pictures but just quick and easy outlines. Ask them to draw as many pictures of a house as they can in one minute. Count the children in so that they are ready: '5, 4, 3, 2, 1, go!'

At the end of one minute, ask the children to count how many houses they have drawn. This could be played as a competition to win small prizes or simply for fun. Set the children other one-minute challenges, such as the suggestions below.

- How many times can you write your name on a piece of paper?
- How many times can you hop on one leg?
- Draw a picture of a cat (show the children a simple picture first).
- How many times can you jump up and down?
- How many times can you throw and catch a ball? (This challenge can be carried out individually, in pairs, or in small groups.)
- How many star jumps can you do?
- How many times can you repeat a phrase such as 'The weather is warm and sunny' to a friend?

Helpful hint

Vary the activity so that written or drawn, physical and spoken activities are used, giving children a fair chance to do well at something.

*

JESUS' BAPTISM

Story reference: Luke 3:1–20; Matthew 3:21–23

River Jordan

Age banding
4–7 (Reception to Year 3)

Aim
To remind the children of what took place when Jesus was baptised.

You will need
The tune for the well-known rhyme 'London Bridge is falling down'.

How to play
Ask the children if they know the rhyme 'London Bridge is falling down'. Hum through the song to familiarise the children with the tune. Explain that you are going to teach different words to this tune, to tell the story of Jesus' baptism.

Verse 1
Jesus looked for Cousin John,
Cousin John, Cousin John.
Jesus looked for Cousin John
by the River Jordan.

Verse 2

John baptised him with a splash,
with a splash, with a splash.
John baptised him with a splash
in the River Jordan.

Verse 3

A dove came down, God spoke from heaven,
spoke from heaven, spoke from heaven.
A dove came down, God spoke from heaven
by the River Jordan.

Once the children have mastered the words, ask them to stand in a circle, facing inwards, with gaps between them. Ask one child to stand in the centre of the circle. This child is going to be 'Jesus'. Now ask each child to form an archway with a child next to them by turning towards each other, joining both hands and holding them high in the air.

Explain that as you all sing, 'Jesus' is going to wind in and out of the circle, passing quickly through each archway in turn. When you get to the last line of each verse, the children need to be ready, as on the word 'Jordan' the archways are going to bring their arms down and Jesus will be caught as he or she passes through.

The two children who caught Jesus now form a line behind him, carefully holding on to his waist. Jesus then leads the two children through the archways as the second verse is sung. Again the archways bring down their arms on the word 'Jordan'. If anyone catches a child, their archway joins on to the line and the third verse is sung, with the archways bringing down their arms in the same way. The game can then be repeated with a different child being Jesus.

Helpful hint

If the class numbers are small, simply have a circle of children standing with gaps between them, and ask 'Jesus' to wind in and out of the children. On the word 'Jordan', the children that Jesus is passing between join on to the back of him, and the game continues.

Cross over

Age banding

7–11 (Years 3 to 6)
All ages

Aim

To remind the children that John baptised Jesus in the River Jordan.

You will need

Something to mark out two lines, such as chairs, tape, coats and so on; a music CD and CD player (optional); stickers or small pieces of paper.

How to play

Mark the room into three areas.

River Jordan

Ask the children to stand in one of the end areas. Explain that the central area is the River Jordan and that the children are going to try to get across it. If you have music available, the children begin to cross when the music starts. The children walk 'across the Jordan' and into the area marked at the opposite end of the room. Once in that area, they can only stay for five seconds and then they must cross back again. Once they reach the first area, they can only stay there for five seconds before crossing the Jordan again. (There is no need for the children to wait five seconds; they can run backwards and forwards immediately if they like.)

If any children are in the Jordan when the music stops, they are given a sticker or a small piece of paper. They then continue in the game. At the end of the game, the children count how many stickers or pieces of paper they have. The child with the fewest is the winner.

If there is no music available, a leader, facing away from the children, can shout 'Go!' and 'Stop!' to start and end each round.

Helpful hint

Once the children understand the game, add additional instructions such as crossing the Jordan by hopping, jumping, crawling and so on.

*

JESUS' DISCIPLES

Story reference: Matthew 4:18–22; Luke 5:1–11, 27–32; John 1:43–50

Name five

Age banding
4–7 (Reception to Year 3)
All ages

Aim
To remind the children that the disciples had to work together as a team when they began to follow Jesus.

How to play
Ask the children to stand in a circle, facing inwards. Give one child the ball. Explain that you are going to call out a letter of the alphabet and the child holding the ball has to name five things beginning with that letter before the ball has been passed round the circle and back to him or her. For example, if Kelly is holding the ball and you call out the letter 'B', Kelly will pass the ball to the child next to her, who will continue to pass it round the circle as quickly as possible. At the same time, Kelly may call out, 'Ball, bat,

bed, banana, butterfly'. If you called the letter 'R', Kelly might say, 'Rabbit, road, rat, radish, roof'.

Whether or not the child manages five answers in the time taken for the ball to travel round the circle, a different child begins with the ball for the next game, until each child has had a turn.

Helpful hint

If there are a lot of children playing the game, you may want to ask for more than five objects to be named. If only a few children are playing, ask for fewer than five objects to be named or spread the circle out so that there are bigger gaps between the children when they pass the ball.

People pairs

Age banding

7–11 (Years 3 to 6)

Aim

To remind the children of people in the Bible who often appear in pairs, such as Jesus' disciples James and John. Friendship and support is very important.

You will need

16 sheets of A4 paper, each cut into four pieces.

Write each of the following words on two of the pieces of paper.

James	John	Mary	Joseph
Boaz	Ruth	Paul	Silas
Mary	Martha	Priscilla	Aquila
Samson	Delilah	Cain	Abel
Abraham	Sarah	Isaac	Rebekah
Barnabas	Mark	Sarah	Zechariah
Adam	Eve	David	Goliath
Ananias	Sapphira	Jacob	Esau

How to play

Split the children into two teams and ask them to line up against the walls at opposite ends of the room. Place the pieces of paper on the floor in the middle of the room, an equal distance from both teams and with the words showing.

On your signal, one child from each team runs to the centre and collects two pieces of paper that they think are a matching pair of people from the Bible. The child takes the pair back to their team and, if they agree that the pair matches, another child runs to the middle to collect a different pair. The game continues until the first team has collected all 16 pairs and the pairs are lined up for the leader to check. The other team continues to play the game until a leader has checked the pairs, as, if any are incorrect, the game continues until one team completes the task correctly.

Helpful hints

- To make the game more difficult, turn the pairs so the words face downwards in the centre of the room. The children then have to search for the matching pair.
- When the leader checks the pairs towards the end of the game, they should point out which pairs are incorrect so that the children don't change answers they have already got right.

*

MIRACLE: JESUS WALKS ON WATER

Story reference: Matthew 14:22–33; Mark 6:45–52; John 6:16–21

Remove your shoes

Age banding
4–7 (Reception to Year 3)

Aim
To remind the children that Jesus walked on the water but Peter began to sink when he tried to do the same.

You will need

No equipment is needed.

How to play
Ask all the children to sit in a circle with a small gap between each child. Explain that you want them to take off their shoes and place them in a big pile in the middle of the circle. Mix the shoes up so that they are in a muddle. Now ask for a volunteer. Explain that they need to put the shoes into pairs and place them in front of the child whom they think the shoes belong to. (They place their own shoes in the gap where they were sitting.)

While the shoes are being placed, the owners of the shoes must keep quiet and not indicate if the shoes have been placed correctly or not. When all the shoes have been placed in front of a child, explain that you are going to count to three, after which you want the children to shout 'Yes' if the shoes placed in front of them are their own, and 'No' if they have been given the incorrect shoes. If any child shouts 'No', all the shoes are placed back in the middle and a different child has a go at sorting the shoes.

Helpful hint

A variation to this game is that when the sorter places the pair of shoes in front of the first child, they say, 'I think these shoes are yours.' If the child says 'Yes', he or she puts on the shoes and becomes the sorter, while the original sorter returns to their place. If, after the statement, 'I think these shoes are yours', the child says 'No', the shoes are placed back in the middle and the sorter must select a different pair of shoes and ask a different child.

Cross the water

Age banding
7–11 (Years 3 to 6)
All ages

Aim
To help the children remember that Jesus walked on the water.

You will need

Stepping stones made out of large pieces of paper or card, paper towels, carpet tiles or sheets of newspaper (enough for one per child); either four chairs or stickers, or a piece of chalk to make a chalk line.

How to play

Split the children into teams of approximately six. Place one stepping stone in the centre of the room and then pace out four equal distances from the centre and place a marker (chair, sticker or chalk line) at each of the four positions. Make the distances as long as possible. Ask each team to stand behind a marker.

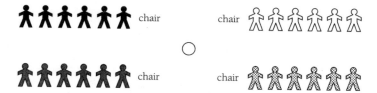

Ask one child from each team to stand on the stepping stone in the middle of the playing area. These children are acting as Peter, who needed rescuing by Jesus. Give one stepping stone to each member of each team, apart from the child in the middle.

The aim of the game is for each team to move to the centre of the room, rescue their player and bring them back home to behind the marker from which they started. They must end with all the stepping stones in a neat pile behind the start marker. The children can only step on the stepping stones, not on the actual floor.

The children will need to work out that the first player needs to place their stepping stone on the floor and stand on it. They then need to be given the next stepping stone so that they can place it in front of the first and then step on to it while they position the third stepping stone and so on. The rest of the team will need to work together to pass the stepping stones and to move forward.

When all the stones are used, the team will need to squash up to release the back stepping stone, enabling it to be passed to the front of the line to continue the journey. The journey home is slightly more difficult as the children will need to squash up more as 'Peter' will be with them.

Helpful hints

- For smaller numbers, time the rescue journey and challenge the children to complete the task in a quicker time.
- Many carpet shops will give away old carpet samples or sell them cheaply: they are really useful for quick games.

*

MIRACLE: JESUS HEALS A CRIPPLED MAN

Story reference: Mark 2:1–12; Luke 5:17–26

Swap the friend

Age banding
4–7 (Reception to Year 3)

Aim
To remind the children that the crippled man had good friends who carried him to see Jesus.

You will need

No equipment is needed.

How to play
Place the children in pairs and ask them to space themselves out over the playing area. Explain that you are going to give them a series of instructions to carry out with their partners, but whenever you call out 'Swap the friend' they must go and find a new partner and carry out your instructions with that partner.

Instructions might include the following:

- Stand back to back.
- One person sit on the other's knee.

- Link arms.
- One person do ten star jumps while the other counts.
- Slap your knees and then clap hands with your partner ten times.
- Make your partner laugh.
- Work out a balance with each partner, with only one foot each on the floor.

Helpful hints

- It is often better to place children into pairs rather than asking them to choose partners. This stops some children from feeling left out.
- If there is an odd number of children, place one set of children in a trio.

Carry your mat!

Age banding

7–11 (Years 3 to 6)
All ages

Aim

To remind the children that Jesus performed a great miracle when he told the crippled man to take up his mat and walk.

You will need

One piece of paper per child (this can be any kind of paper but all the pieces must be the same size); music CD and CD player (optional).

How to play

Give each child a piece of paper. Explain that you are going to ask them to move around the room until the music stops (or you say 'stop'). Then each child must place their piece of paper on the floor and stand on it. They must have no part of their feet over the edge of the paper: you will wander round and check.

When you call out, 'Pick up your mat', the children must pick up their paper and fold it in half. They continue to move round until the music stops and then place their folded piece of paper on the floor and stand on it. The children can stand on tiptoe or balance on one leg but no part of their foot can be touching the floor when you check.

The game continues, with the children folding their mats smaller and smaller, until a 'champion mat-balancer' is found. All the children continue with the game even if they don't manage to balance on a particular size of mat. Sometimes they improve as they see how other children carry out their balances.

Helpful hint

If larger pieces of paper, such as sheets of newspaper, are available, this game is fun carried out in pairs. Two children walk around the room together and, when the music stops, both children have to work together to balance on the mat. The paper is then folded as above and the game continues.

---

*

MIRACLE: JESUS AND BARTIMAEUS

Story reference: Luke 18:35–43; Mark 10:46–52

Blind drop

Age banding
4–7 (Reception to Year 3)

Aim
To remind the children that it can be difficult to know what is happening when you can't see.

You will need

A selection of ten objects collected quickly (these objects must be suitable for dropping on a table—for example, scissors, hat, shoe, pencil, plastic cup, rubber, ball, packet of crisps, beanbag, sticky tape, paperclip and so on); something to provide a screen, such as a large piece of paper, table on its side, chair with a coat over or similar; sheet of paper and pencil (optional).

How to play
Show the children the selection of objects and, if possible, write them down or quickly draw them so that the children can remember what they are. Talk about how people with visual disabilities need

to be able to listen very carefully to things going on around them, as they are often unable to see what is happening. Explain that you are going to drop the objects, one at a time, on to the floor or a table. You want the children to listen very carefully and see if they can guess which item you dropped.

Set up a screen so that the children can't see the item being dropped. Stop after each item has been dropped and see if the children can guess verbally what it is. Repeat the dropping if they need help.

Turn the activity into a team game by splitting the children into small teams and recording the answers on a piece of paper after the team discussion.

Helpful hint

Try to choose a few items that will be easy to guess, such as a bunch of keys, to begin the game while the children get the hang of it.

No peeping

Age banding
7–11 (Years 3 to 6)
All ages

Aim
To help the children realise that not being able to see sometimes means that you have no idea who has touched you.

You will need

No equipment is needed.

How to play

Choose three children to stand at the front while the rest of the children remain seated. On your instruction, all the seated children must shut their eyes, put their heads down and place their hands in the air with their thumbs sticking up. The three children at the front now walk quietly round, gently squeeze the thumbs of one person each and return to their places at the front. If a child's thumbs are squeezed, they should tuck their thumbs inside their hands so that they are not chosen by someone else.

Once the three 'squeezers' have returned to the front, tell the other children that they can now look up. Ask those children whose thumbs were squeezed to put their hands up.

Each child with their hand up has one guess as to which child squeezed their thumbs. If a child guesses correctly, they swap places with the child at the front who squeezed them. If a child guesses incorrectly, they remain in their seat and the person at the front continues as the 'squeezer'. The game is repeated as many times as needed.

Helpful hint

If there are lots of children, ask more of them to be at the front as 'squeezers'.

*

MIRACLE: JESUS AND LAZARUS

Story reference: John 11:1–44

Expressions

Age banding
4–7 (Reception to Year 3)

Aim
To remind the children that Jesus had many different feelings when he was on earth. In this story he cried when his friend died.

You will need
No equipment is needed.

How to play
Ask the children to sit in a circle, facing inwards, with a gap between each person. Explain that you are going to pick a child to start the game. They need to stand up and move so that they are standing in front of another child. They then need to pull a face that shows some emotion to the seated child. It may be that they look very angry, they start to cry, they laugh hysterically and so on. The child who has pulled the face now sits in the place of the seated child, and the seated child stands up and moves to pull the same face to a different child.

If a child laughs, either while they pull the face or while they have a face pulled at them, a different person is chosen to begin a new game by pulling a face showing a different emotion at another child.

Helpful hint

Choose a child who is likely to pull a funny face to get the game started. Once the children have started laughing, they find the game much more difficult.

Lazarus, come out!

Age banding
7–11 (Years 3 to 6)
All ages

Aim
To remind the children that Jesus raised Lazarus from the dead.

You will need

Chairs (one per child).

How to play
Split the children into two teams of six to eight players. Arrange the chairs to make two enclosures (tombs) with a hole for a door. The chairs should be facing outwards. Place the tombs as far away from each other as possible, with enough room for the children to move round the outside of them.

Set up   Game

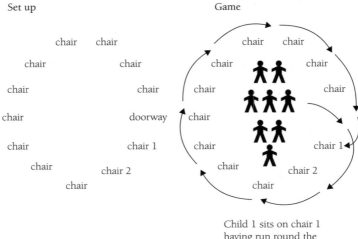

Child 1 sits on chair 1
having run round the
circle and past the doorway

Ask all the children to sit inside their 'tomb'. Explain that, on your instruction, the first team member is going to come out of the tomb, run all the way round the tomb, pass the tomb entrance and then sit down on the first chair (marked 1). When the first player sits down, the second child comes out of the tomb, runs round the tomb, passes the tomb entrance and sits on the chair marked 2 and so on. The chairs must be filled in order. The game continues until the last child sits on a chair. At this point all the team shouts together, 'Empty!'

Helpful hint

The game can be repeated, asking the children to jump round the tomb, hop round the tomb and so on. If space is limited, one tomb could be set up and the teams timed to see who could empty the tomb the quickest.

*

PARABLE: A STORY ABOUT A FARMER

Story reference: Luke 8:4–15

Keep the seed tray full!

Age banding
4–7 (Reception to Year 3)

Aim
To remind the children that, in the story about a farmer, some of the birds came and ate the seeds that were sown.

You will need
A container, such as a bowl, box or bag; five pieces of A4 paper cut in to four and screwed into small balls (20 balls will be made).

How to play
Ask all the children to stand round the outside of the room. Position yourself in the centre of the room with the box full of 'seeds' in front of you. Explain that you are going to be the farmer sowing the seed. You will throw out one seed at a time and the children have to collect that seed and place it back into the box. However, as soon as you have thrown one seed, you will throw another into a different part of the room, followed by another, then another and so on. Your aim is to empty the box of all the seeds. The children's

aim is to make sure that you don't! After a while, you may like to have a child to be the farmer sowing the seed.

Helpful hint

It doesn't matter which child retrieves the seeds, but try to throw some seeds close to children who don't seem to be getting any. If a child is playing the part of the farmer, you may like to change the rules and allow them to throw two seeds at once so that they have more chance of emptying their basket.

Seed storm

Age banding
7–11 (Years 3 to 6)
All ages

Aim
To remind the children that the farmer scattered the seed but much of it didn't grow.

You will need

A4 paper cut into six pieces and crumpled up to make about 50 'seeds' (the more seeds, the more fun); masking tape or chalk to make a line.

How to play
Place a line across the playing area, dividing the room in half. Split the children into two teams and ask one team to stand on either side of the line.

Split the 'seed' into two piles and scatter one pile on either side of the central line. Explain that the aim of the game is to 'sow' as much seed as possible on to the opposite team's 'field' but to allow as little as possible on to your own field. When you shout 'Go', the children pick up their seed and throw it on to the opposite side. As seeds land on the opposite side, the teams pick them up and throw them back. This continues until you shout 'Stop!' (Sometimes a whistle is better, as the game can get noisy.)

The children must not throw after the end of the game has been called. If they do, the seed they threw must be returned to their own side. The winning team is the side with the least amount of seed on it. The seed can then be roughly divided in half again and placed on either side of the line for the game to be repeated.

Helpful hint

If you have a lot of children and a lot of space, divide the room into four sections and play the game with four teams.

PARABLE: THE STORY OF THE GOOD SAMARITAN

Story reference: Luke 10:25–37

Funny people

Age banding
4–7 (Reception to Year 3)
All ages

Aim
To remind the children that everybody is different but God cares for us all.

You will need

Paper and pencils.

How to play
Give each child a piece of paper and ask them to secretly draw somebody's head and a bit of their neck in the top third of the paper. The pictures can be as silly as they like—in fact, the funnier, the better. Make sure they don't show anyone.

When everyone has finished, ask the children to fold their papers over so that just the bottom bit of the neck is showing, and swap papers with someone else. On their new paper, ask them (without looking at the head) to secretly draw a body connected to the neck, in the second third of the paper. Point out that just the top bit of the legs should also be drawn. Ask them to fold their papers over so that the legs are showing and again swap their papers.

Finally, ask the children to draw in the legs and feet and then fold their papers so that nothing can be seen. Ask the children to swap their papers one last time and take turns at opening them to reveal the pictures. The children will find them very funny!

Helpful hint

For young children, fold the papers into three before the game begins. This will show them how much of the paper should be used for each section of the drawing.

Long walk

Age banding
7–11 (Years 3 to 6)

Aim
To remind the children that, in the story of the good Samaritan, the man was walking on the road from Jerusalem to Jericho.

You will need

Something to mark a finishing line, such as a rope, tape or chairs; a watch or clock with a second hand.

How to play
Ask all the children to line up at one end of the room. Explain that they are in 'Jerusalem'. Show them the marked area and explain

that they are going to go on a walk from Jerusalem to the marked area—'Jericho'.

Jerusalem

Jericho

Explain that the journey should take exactly two minutes. The time starts when you say 'Go'. The children can walk wherever they want around the room but they need to concentrate as they go, because they are aiming to cross the line into Jericho exactly two minutes after they set out. A child may decide to walk very slowly in a forward direction throughout the two minutes, or they might stand still for a while before continuing forward, or they may walk quickly backwards and forwards all over the room. It doesn't matter what they do, as long as they cross the line at the right time.

Secretly make a note of which child crosses at the two-minute mark but let the other children carry on until all of them have finished. Announce who was the closest to two minutes and then let the children play again.

Helpful hints

- Children love this game if the leaders join in—often, the children do much better than their leaders.
- This is a good game as the fastest or most sporty child may well not win, and the child who finishes first is often not the winner. If you have extra leaders, you may be able to record when each child crosses the line. The children can then enjoy the challenge of bettering their time.

PARABLE: A STORY ABOUT TWO SONS

Story reference: Luke 15:11–32

Squeaking piggy

Age banding
4–7 (Reception to Year 3)
All ages

Aim
To remind the children that the younger son was feeding pigs when he came back to his senses and decided to go home to his father.

You will need
A blindfold.

How to play
Ask the children to stand in a circle with one child in the middle. Gently place the blindfold round this child. Ask the children in the circle to swap positions. Ask the blindfolded child to put their arms out in front of them and find a child standing in the circle. (The children can't run away.) When the child finds someone in the circle, they hold on to them and say 'Squeak, piggy, squeak.' The child in the circle has to squeak like a pig and the blindfolded child has to guess who it is. If they guess incorrectly, they move on

to another child and ask them to 'Squeak, piggy, squeak'. When the child has guessed someone correctly, a different child has a turn in the middle.

Helpful hint

To make the game slightly easier, each child could be allowed three guesses at who squeaked.

Going home

Age banding
7–11 (Years 3 to 6)
All ages

Aim
To reinforce the story of the lost son.

You will need

One chair per child, plus two extra; the story outline below.

How to play
Position the chairs in two rows, facing forward with a gap between each chair. Place an extra chair about one metre away from the last chair. Carefully place the children into teams. The children sitting opposite each other are going to play against each other, so they need to be of similar age or ability. It is easiest to pick children individually. For example, 'Nathan, you are here on chair 1 and, Joel, you are in this team on chair 1'. (Nathan and Joel will be of

a similar standard.) 'Angela, you are number 2 on this team and, Becky, you are 2 on this team.' (Angela and Becky will be of similar standard but might be completely different from the standard of Nathan and Joel.)

Once the children are in teams, explain that you are going to give them all the name of a character in the story of the lost son. Number 1 in both teams will be the same character, as will number 2 in both teams, and so on. Everyone must remember their character names. (The most running will be done by the father and younger son, 2 and 3, so you may like to give those parts to certain children.)

1 Jesus
2 Father
3 Younger son
4 Older son
5 Servant(s)
6 Friends
7 Farmer
8 Pig(s)

Explain that you are going to tell a story. When the children hear the name of their character, they need to run out of the side of their line, round the front of the line, all the way round the chair at the back of their line, down the other side of their line and back into their seat (see example below for player 3). The player who arrives at their seat first receives a point for their team.

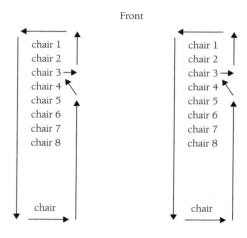

Front

Story

Pause after the names of the characters (shown in bold type). While the running takes place, the game tends to get hectic and noisy.

Jesus loved to tell his followers stories to show them what God, his **Father**, was like. One day he told a wonderful story about an **older son**, a **younger son** and their **father**. This is the story that **Jesus** told.

Once there was a **father** who had two sons. One day the **younger son** came to his **father**.

'**Father**,' he said. 'Please will you give me all the money that I shall get when you die? I want it now. I don't want to wait!'

The **father** was very upset. He knew that his **friends** would think it was wrong of him to let his **younger son** go, but, after some thought, he did what his **younger son** asked. He knew that his **older son** would stay at home and help him and, after all, he did have a lot of **servants** who worked hard for him. The **father** collected all his money and, sadly, he and the **older son** waved goodbye as the **younger son** left home and went off on his travels.

As the **younger son** walked along, he thought about all the fun he was going to have. He was sure he would soon make loads of **friends**. On his way, he walked past a smelly farm. He turned his nose up. He couldn't understand how anyone would be a **farmer** on a **pig** farm. He knew he would never be a **farmer**… especially now that he had so much money. He held his nose until he had gone past the **pigs**.

Soon the **younger son** arrived in the town. He quickly found somewhere to live and hired some **servants** to help him. Before long, **friends** were flocking round him. For a while, the **younger son** didn't even think about his **father** or his brother, the **older son**. He didn't think about anything except having a good time with his **friends** and bossing his **servants** around.

Then suddenly the unthinkable happened! The **younger son** went to pay for something he wanted to buy, but he had no money. He had spent every penny of it. He rushed to his **friends** to see if they would lend him some. However, his **friends** simply turned up their noses. They weren't really his **friends**; they had only liked him for his money. He tried to borrow money from his **servants**, but they wouldn't do anything to help either.

In desperation the **younger son** had an idea. Slowly, he walked towards the farm he had seen on his way to the town. He spotted the **farmer** in the field.

'Excuse me,' he asked the **farmer**. 'Please would you give me a job?'

The **farmer** agreed to give him a job. 'You can feed the **pigs**,' he said.

The **younger son** collected the **pig** food and walked towards the **pigs**. How things had changed in just a short time!

Jesus paused in his story. He could see that the entire crowd were listening intently, so **Jesus** continued.

Day after day, the **younger son** worked for the **farmer**. Day after day, he fed the smelly **pigs**. He grew more and more unhappy. He was so hungry that he even ate the **pig** food when the **farmer** wasn't looking. Then one day he suddenly had an idea.

'I know!' he thought. 'Back at my **father's** house, even the **servants** have enough food, yet here I am, starving. If I go home, maybe my **father** will take me on as one of his **servants**. At least then I won't be starving like I am here with the **pigs**.'

So the **younger son** set off. He said goodbye to the **farmer**. He said goodbye to the **pigs** and he headed for home.

As he walked along, the **younger son** wondered how his brother, the **older son**, would feel when he arrived home. He knew that his brother, the **older son**, had not been happy when he had left. He wondered how he would treat him when he worked as a **servant** in the house.

After a long journey, the **younger son** spotted his home in the distance. He felt nervous. He felt embarrassed. As he got nearer, he looked up. In the distance he could see someone running towards him. He was sure it wasn't one of his **friends**. He was sure it wasn't the **older son**. Suddenly he realised who it was. It was his **father**.

The **father** threw his arms round his son's neck. Immediately the **younger son** asked if he could be taken back as a **servant**, but his **father** refused. Instead, he ordered the **servants** to make a special meal. He ordered that special clothes be brought and invited all his family and **friends** to a huge party. The **servants** got busy at once.

As he climbed into bed that night, the **younger son** thought of everything his **father** had done for him. He thought of the **farmer** and the smelly **pigs**. He thought of all those people he had believed to be his **friends**, who had turned away from him when he was in need. He thought of his brother, the **older son**. He knew his brother was not happy that he had been welcomed home like this. Deep down, the **younger son** knew he didn't deserve to be treated well. He couldn't understand the forgiveness of his **father**.

Jesus finished his story and looked round at the crowd. He felt rather sad. **Jesus** knew that lots of them didn't understand the story. **Jesus** desperately wanted the people to understand how much God, his **Father**, wanted to forgive them.

So there is the story that **Jesus** told about his **Father**. A story about a **younger son** and an **older son**; a story about **farmers**, **servants**, **friends** and, of course, some **pigs**!

Helpful hints

- Have another helper keeping the score, as it is hard to score and read at the same time.
- If you have more children, have more teams.

PARABLE: A STORY ABOUT TWO BUILDERS

Story reference: Matthew 7:24–27

Big house, little house

Age banding

4–7 (Reception to Year 3)

Aim

To remind the children about the story of the two builders.

You will need
No equipment is needed.

How to play

Ask all the children to sit in a semicircle with you at the front.

Explain that you are going to say certain words while doing certain actions. The children must do the correct action for the thing you say, not the action you do. You are going to say the words 'Big house'. When you do, you will move your hands together, palms pointing at each other, to show a small house. When you say the words 'Little house', you will move your hands apart as if indicating a big house. No matter what action you do, the children should always act out the action for the spoken words.

This game can be played for fun or children who get it wrong can remain in the circle and watch until a winner is found.

Helpful hint

You can make this game more active by changing the actions. Standing up as tall as possible with hands in the air could indicate a big house, and rolling up on the floor in a ball could indicate a little house. You could introduce other actions such as 'Wobbly foundations' (all the children tremble like jelly) or 'Windy day' (all the children run round) and so on.

Knock it down

Age banding
7–11 (Years 3 to 6)
All ages

Aim
To remind the children about the importance of a firm foundation.

You will need

One chair per child plus two extra; two things to throw, such
as sponge balls, beanbags (if available) or pairs of socks rolled
together to make a ball; something to knock down, such as
empty plastic bottles, two pieces of A4 paper bent into cone
shapes, or old books standing on their ends.

How to play

Place two lines of chairs opposite each other, as far apart as possible.
Split the children into two teams and ask them to sit on the chairs.
Number each child, starting with '1' at opposite ends. The children
must remember their number. Place a chair in the middle at each
end, with the balls (or equivalent) placed on them. Place the target
in the centre. Tell the children which is their team's chair.

Chair A

Team A		Team B
1		8
2		7
3		6
4	●	5
5	target	4
6		3
7		2
8		1

Chair B

Explain that you are going to call out a number. If you call 'Number
6', child 6 from each team must run to their chair, place one knee
on the chair with the other foot on the ground and throw the ball
at the target. If both children miss the target, they run and collect
the nearest ball, return to their chair and try again. This continues

until one child has hit the target, which results in one point for that team. The balls are placed back on the chairs and a different number is called.

Helpful hint

Keep track of which numbers you have called so that the children get a fair number of turns. They will be quick to tell you if they don't!

---

*

MARY AND MARTHA

Story reference: Luke 10:38–42

This and that

Age banding
4–7 (Reception to Year 3)
All ages

Aim
To remind the children that Martha was always busy and didn't always listen.

How to play
Ask all the children to stand facing you. Explain that you are going to do all sorts of different actions. (Give some examples, such as standing on one leg, scratching your head and so on.) If you say, 'Do this', you want the children to copy the action you are doing. However, if you say the words 'Do that', you don't want the children to copy.

For example, you say, 'Do this' while hopping on one leg. All the children should follow you. You say, 'Do this' whilst pointing your toes. All the children stop hopping and point their toes. You say, 'Do this' while nodding your head. All the children stop pointing their toes and nod their heads. You say, 'Do that' while doing star jumps. All the children should ignore you and continue to nod their heads.

Helpful hint

Use some actions that could specifically refer to Martha, such as sweeping, scrubbing the floor, cooking and so on. Young children like to have a go at being the leader for this game and often have more original ideas for different actions to do.

Which woman?

Age banding
7–11 (Years 3 to 6)

Aim
To remind the children of the story of Mary and Martha.

You will need

One chair per child.

How to play
Ask the children to place their chairs in a circle and sit on them, facing inwards. Make a gap at one point in the circle. Number the chairs from 1 to however many children are playing the game (this game works with between six and 20 children).

Fill the Gap!

                    Chair 4

            Chair 5   Chair 3

          Chair 6   Chair 2

      Chair 7   Chair 1

          Chair 8

            Chair 9   Chair 11

                  Chair 10

Before you begin the game, the children need to learn what to say. The leader says the following rhyme.

One woman was busy, one just sat,
Some say this and some say that,
But I say number …

When a child's number is called, they must jump up and say, 'Who, me?' The leader then says, 'Yes, you!' They say, 'Not me!' The leader says, 'Then who?' They say, 'Number …'.

The child whose number has just been called jumps up and says, 'Who, me?' The leader then says, 'Yes, you!' The child says, 'Not me!' The leader says, 'Then who?' The child says, 'Number …'.

So the game repeats. If a child says their number wrong or gets their words confused or jumps up too slowly, they have to move on to the end chair (number 11 in the diagram above). To allow this to happen, all the children with a higher number than the child who needs to move must move along. At this point, they will change their number to the number of the chair they have moved to. So if number 5 has moved to chair 11, 6 becomes 5, 7 becomes 6, 8 becomes 7, 9 becomes 8, 10 becomes 9 and 11 becomes 10. The numbers below 5 do not move, as there should not be a chair for them to move on to. The aim of the game is to be in position 1 when the game ends.

Make it clear to the children that it is the chair that is numbered, *not* the child. They will stay with the number they have been given until they move to a different chair.

For example:

Leader:
One woman was busy, one just sat,
Some say this and some say that,
But I say number 3.

Number 3:	Who, me?
Leader:	Yes, you!
Number 3:	Not me!
Leader:	Then who?
Number 3:	Number 7.
Number 7:	Who, me?
Leader:	Yes, you!
Number 7:	Not me!
Leader:	Then who?
Number 7:	Number 1.
Number 1:	Who, me?
Leader:	Yes, you!
Number 1:	Not me!
Leader:	Then who?
Number 1:	Number 2.

Number 2 isn't listening so doesn't stand up. Then you say 'Too slow! Move to the back.' Number 2 moves to number 11 and numbers 3–11 all move down a number. Number 1 stays the same.

The leader now begins again with the rhyme for the next round.

Helpful hint

If possible, stick labels on the chairs so that it is easy for the children to identify what their number is when they move. When a child moves to the last seat and the leader repeats the rhyme, he or she uses the opportunity to say the number of a child who has not yet had a turn.

*

ZACCHAEUS

Story reference: Luke 19:1–10

Thief!

Age banding
4–7 (Reception to Year 3)
All ages

Aim
To remind the children that Zacchaeus stole money from the people around him before Jesus changed his life.

You will need

A roll of paper made from either a sheet of A3 rolled lengthways or two pieces of A4 stuck together lengthways; a beanbag, keys, book or similar to represent 'treasure'; a blindfold, such as a scarf or hat (or you can trust the child to keep his or her eyes closed).

How to play
Ask all the children to sit in a circle with a small gap between them. Ask one child to sit in the centre of the circle, and place the blindfold on this child. Place the 'treasure' on the floor in front of the central child and ask them to hold the roll of paper.

Explain that you are going to point to one child in the circle. They will stand up and sneak towards the central child with the aim of stealing the treasure. The central child is not allowed to move from the spot on which they are sitting but will use the roll of paper to try to touch the 'thief' before he or she takes the treasure.

Helpful hint

If there are two leaders (or older children) available, it is helpful to demonstrate some tactics for this game before the children have a go. The thief can watch carefully to see how the central child moves the roll of paper. For example, if they are just waving it high, the thief could crawl to avoid being hit. If they are just waving it in front of them, the thief could approach from behind, and so on.

Grab the bag

Age banding
7–11 (Years 3 to 6)

Aim
To remind the children that Zacchaeus was a tax collector who stole money from people until Jesus changed his life.

You will need

A money bag (an old-fashioned money bag is ideal but any small bag will do, or even something to represent a bag, such as a tea towel or plastic bottle); one chair per child, or two lines marked on the floor.

How to play

Divide the children into two equal teams. Set out two lines of chairs (one per person) opposite each other, approximately 6–8m apart. Ask the teams to sit on the chairs and place the bag in the middle.

1   2   3   4   5   6   7   8   9   10

●

10   9   8   7   6   5   4   3   2   1

Number each child, starting with '1' at opposite ends. Explain that when you call out their number, a child from each team has to run to the middle, grab the money bag and return to their chair. If they manage to do this, they get a point. However, once a child has the bag, the other child must run after them, and, if they make contact before the child with the bag sits down, the point becomes theirs. The children do not have to grab the bag immediately. They can wait and walk round the bag, weighing up their opponent before the grab is made.

Helpful hint
If there are lots of children, the chairs can be arranged in a square, with opposite teams playing each other and two bags in the middle.

＊

PALM SUNDAY

Story reference: Matthew 21:1–11; Mark 11:1–11; Luke 19:28–44; John 12:12–19

Donkey

Age banding
4–7 (Reception to Year 3)
All ages

Aim
To remind the children of Jesus' entry into Jerusalem.

You will need
No equipment is needed.

How to play
This is a movement game in which the children respond by making appropriate actions when you call out certain colours. Teach the children the actions that you would like them to make in response to your words, as follows:

- **Green:** stand still with arms outstretched (Palm tree).
- **Grey:** get on the floor and crawl on all fours (Donkey moving).
- **Red:** move around room quickly—run if room allows, or walk fast if there is less space (people running to see Jesus).

- **Orange:** stand on tiptoe and walk round as if looking for someone (crowd trying to spot Jesus).
- **Donkey:** children get into pairs, with one child kneeling down and the other child sitting carefully on their back.

When the children know the actions, begin to call out the colours and give time for the children to respond. When the word 'Donkey' is shouted, the children must pair up with the child nearest to them. You may want to play the game simply for fun or you can give the quickest pair to get into position a sticker (or piece of cut-up paper) so that the child with the most stickers at the end of the game is the winner. The game can be repeated as many times as needed, and the children will enjoy having a turn at calling out the words.

Helpful hint

You may like to ask the children to make up their own actions for the colours above, or even encourage them to suggest different colours and actions to do with the story of Palm Sunday.

Catch the donkey's tail

Age banding
7–11 (Years 3 to 6)

Aim
To remind the children that Jesus made his entry into Jerusalem riding on a donkey.

You will need

Strips of fabric or paper.

How to play

Give every child a strip of fabric or paper approximately 70cm long. Either ask the children to push one end of the strip slightly down the back of their waistband or attach the strip to the child's back with a small piece of sticky tape. The children should now have a 'donkey's tail'. When you say 'Go', the aim of the game is for the children to try to steal each other's tails while keeping their own. If a child manages to get someone else's tail, they keep it in their hand and continue to try to get other people's. If a child's tail is taken, they can still continue to steal tails. The winner is the child with the most tails at the end of the game.

Helpful hint •

Make sure the children don't keep hold of their own tails so that others can't get them.

*

LAST SUPPER

Story reference: John 13:1–30

Where's the shoe?

Age banding
4–7 (Reception to Year 3)

Aim
To remind the children that Jesus removed the disciples' shoes and washed their feet.

You will need
A shoe.

How to play
Ask the children to sit in a tight circle with one child standing in the middle. Give the child in the middle the shoe to hold. Teach the children the words below:

Wash my feet, here's my shoe.
Is there one or is there two?

I know that it is one of you.
Tell me who has got the shoe!

When the children have mastered the words, explain that the central child (child 1) will say the first two lines above:

'Wash my feet, here's my shoe.
Is there one or is there two?'

As the child says these words, he or she will pass the shoe to a child in the circle (child 2). Child 1 will then move back into the middle, shut their eyes and cover them with their hands. Child 2 immediately begins to pass the shoe, behind their back, to the person next them. As the shoe moves round the circle, the children say:

'I know that it is one of you,
Tell me who has got the shoe!'

Whoever is holding the shoe when the word 'shoe!' is spoken retains it, ensuring that it is held out of sight. Child 1 now opens his or her eyes and looks carefully round the circle. Child 1 has two guesses as to who has the shoe. If they guess correctly, they remain in the centre and the game is repeated. If they have not guessed correctly after two turns, the child holding the shoe moves into the middle.

Helpful hint

Children love the leaders squashing into the circle with them. If there are a lot of children, play the game with two shoes so that there is more chance of the central child guessing correctly.

Walking feet

Age banding
7–11 (Years 3 to 6)
All ages

Aim
To remind the children that Jesus showed his love by washing his disciples' feet.

Large footprint shapes cut from paper (or just use sheets of A4 paper); water drop shapes cut out of paper (blue is ideal), with a coil of sticky tape or Blu-tack on the back of each (or just use stickers or post-it notes).

How to play
Divide the children into teams of about six. Mark two lines on the floor and ask the children to line up in their teams behind one line. Place a pile of water drop shapes behind the opposite line. Give each team two footprint shapes.

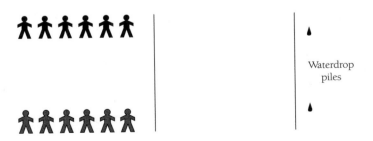

Waterdrop
piles

The aim of the game is for the children to move, one at a time, from one line to the other to collect water drops. Each child has to move without stepping on anything other than the two large footprint shapes. To do this, they need to either stand on the two shapes, bend over, grasp the front of the footprints and pull them forward as they shuffle, or stand on one footprint while placing the other in front of them and stepping on to it.

When the child crosses the opposite line, they must stick one water drop on one of their footprint shapes and then run back to give both footprint shapes to the second in line. The winning team is the first to be seated behind the start line, with the same number of water drops on the footprints as the number of children in their team.

Helpful hint

For younger children, it is good for a leader to demonstrate different ways of moving forward using the footprints before the game begins. Older children tend to like to experiment for themselves.

---

*

EASTER

Story reference: Matthew 26:31—27:66; Mark 14:32—15:47; Luke 22:39—23:56; John 18:1—19:42

We have seen him!

Age banding
4–7 (Reception to Year 3)
All ages

Aim
To remind the children that many people saw Jesus after he had risen from the dead.

You will need
A toy figure or a small figure cut out of paper.

How to play
Show the figure to the children. Explain that they are going to leave the room while you hide the figure somewhere in the room. They will come back into the room and look for the figure. However, when they see it, they will not tell anyone but will simply come and sit down in a designated place. All the other children will continue to look, sitting down when they have seen the figure.

The first child to find it will be the child to hide it for the next game.

Helpful hints

- Try to make sure the children already seated don't point to where the figure is hidden.
- You may like to play so that the last child to spot the figure will be the hider for the next game.

Origami cross trick

Age banding
7–11 (Years 3 to 6)

Aim
To teach the children a simple visual aid that reminds them of the Easter story.

You will need

Sheets of A4 paper (one per child); scissors.

How to play
Give each child a piece of A4 paper and help them to fold it as shown opposite.

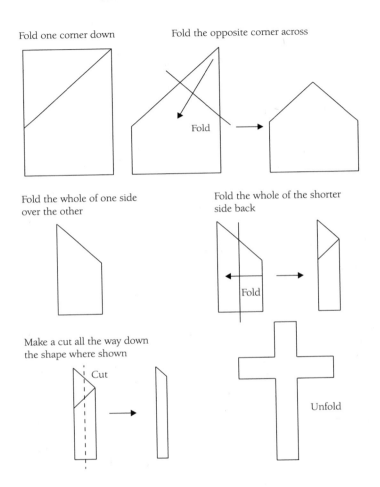

Fold one corner down

Fold the opposite corner across

Fold

Fold the whole of one side over the other

Fold the whole of the shorter side back

Fold

Make a cut all the way down the shape where shown

Cut

Unfold

Helpful hint

To use less paper, small rectangles can be used. You could set a challenge to see who could make the tiniest cross.

*

EASTER

Story reference: Matthew 28:1–15; Mark 16:1–9; Luke 24:1–49; John 20:1–31

Pass the stone

Age banding
4–7 (Reception to Year 3)
All ages

Aim
To remind the children that when the women arrived at the tomb, the stone had been moved.

You will need
A small stone (if a stone is not available, half a piece of A4 paper can be rolled into a stone shape).

How to play
Ask the children to stand in a circle, facing inwards, with a small gap between them. Select one child to stand in the middle. Explain that when the women arrived at the tomb on Easter morning, they were worried because they thought they would have to move the stone away from the entrance. They needn't have worried, though, because an angel had come and moved the stone away for them.

Ask the child in the centre to close their eyes. (Check they are not cheating!) Give the stone to one child and allow the children to start passing the stone and pretending to pass the stone. So that the game is not obvious, all the children need to keep moving their hands to pretend they are passing the stone, even if the real stone is at the opposite side of the circle.

Now ask the central child to open their eyes and watch carefully as the stone is passed round before making a guess as to where the stone is. If the guess is correct, the child who was holding the stone moves into the middle and the original 'guesser' takes their place. If the guess is incorrect, the guesser continues their turn.

Helpful hint

If the guessing is taking too long, allow just three guesses before the child in the centre is swapped.

Can you walk out?

Age banding

7–11 (Years 3 to 6)

Aim

To teach the children a simple paper trick that reminds them of the Easter story.

You will need

A4 paper (one sheet for each child); scissors.

How to play

This game is a paper trick to reinforce the resurrection story. Give each child a piece of A4 paper and ask them to imagine it is a door.

Remind the children that, after Jesus had risen from the dead, he appeared to his disciples many times, often without using the door.

The challenge is to see if the children can use the scissors to make a hole in the paper that is big enough for them to walk through. The hole must be complete: it cannot be stuck together with sticky tape. They can use scissors but nothing else.

Some children will come up with ideas for doing this; some will say it is impossible. Reassure them that it's not! Let them have time to experiment before you help them.

The secret to doing this is to fold the paper in half and cut as shown below. The children will then have a circle large enough for them to walk through.

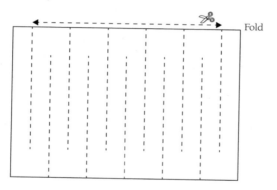

Fold

Helpful hint

By cutting carefully, you can manage to make a hole from a very small rectangle of paper that is big enough to climb through. The children could experiment to see how small a piece of paper they can walk through.

*

JESUS AND PETER

Story reference: John 21:1–25

I draw a sheep

Age banding
4–7 (Reception to Year 3)
All ages

Aim
To remind the children that Jesus forgave Peter and asked him to 'feed his sheep' (to be the leader of the early church).

You will need
No equipment is needed.

How to play
Ask one child to volunteer so that you can demonstrate the game. Explain that you are going to say a rhyme and, at the same time, draw a sheep shape on the child's back. At the end of the rhyme, you will touch the child's back with one finger or thumb. They have to guess which finger you touched them with. The rhyme is as follows.

'I draw a sheep upon your back. With which finger did I touch it?'

While you say, 'I draw a sheep upon your back', continue to draw a sheep shape on the child's back with your finger. When you say, 'With which finger did I touch it?' pause for a moment and touch the child quite definitely with only one finger. Now place both your hands, with your fingers spread out, in front of the child and ask them to guess which finger you touched them with. If they are incorrect, bend that finger under and let them continue to guess until they guess correctly.

Split the children into pairs and tell them which child in each pair is going to do the drawing. Allow them to have a go on each other's backs. You will need to help them say the rhyme at first.

The game is simply for fun. When the children have had a go in one pair, they could swap round to a different child.

Helpful hint

This is a good activity when children don't know each other very well. It gives the children the chance to mingle and have contact with each other without the need to make conversation.

Find the leader

Age banding
7–11 (Years 3 to 6)
All ages

Aim
To remind the children that Jesus accepted Peter as the leader, despite the fact that he had denied knowing Jesus.

You will need

No equipment is needed.

How to play

Ask all the children to sit in a circle. Explain that one child will be asked to leave the room, after which a leader will be selected from the rest of the group. When the child returns to the room, he or she must stand in the centre of the circle. The child chosen as leader will then start off a particular action—for example, flap their wings like the cockerel that crowed as Peter denied Jesus, cry as Peter did when he realised what he had done, fold their fingers together and kneel down as if pleading for forgiveness, and so on. When those in the circle see the action, they must copy the leader immediately.

The child in the centre has to guess who the leader is, while the leader does his or her best not to get caught. When the child in the centre guesses correctly, they take their place in the circle and the leader becomes the central child. This child then leaves the room and a new leader is chosen.

Helpful hint

This game can be played for most Bible stories. The leader is reminded of the story that has been studied and then has to use actions related to the story. For example, the actions for Bartimaeus might be begging, wearing glasses, holding hands in the air to praise and so on; the actions for Zacchaeus might be climbing a tree, putting hand to head to peer up into the tree, rubbing fingers together to indicate lots of money, and so on.

*

ASCENSION

Story reference: Acts 1:1–11

Pass it on

Age banding
4–7 (Reception to Year 3)
All ages

Aim
To remind the children that Jesus asked the disciples to pass on his message to the rest of the world.

You will need
No equipment is needed.

How to play
Ask the children to sit in a circle and think of any words at all that could relate to Jesus or the Bible. (Suitable words could be Lord, Peter, boat, fish, seed, cross, God, disciples, Paul, tent, heal and so on.) Explain that you are going to teach the children a simple series of actions that you want them to follow.

The actions are: pat your knees with your hands... clap your hands together ... click your fingers on one hand, followed by your fingers on the other hand (it doesn't matter if the children can't make a sound when they click their fingers). Try to get a steady rhythm going by repeating the sequence of actions. Explain that everyone will do the actions together but, on the first click, each child in turn will say a 'Bible word'. If the word has two syllables, you will find it easy to say one syllable on the first click and the second syllable on the second click.

For example:

- Pat hands on knees
- Clap hands together
- Click: Pe...
- Click: ... ter
- Pat hands on knees
- Clap hands together
- Click: Disci...
- Click: ... ples
- Pat hands on knees
- Clap hands together
- Click: fish...
- Click: ... es
- Pat hands on knees
- Clap hands together
- Click: crea...
- Click: ... tion

The aim of the game is to get all the way round the circle with each child saying a word. At first it doesn't matter if the children have to repeat the pat, clap and click rhythm a few times while they wait for a child to think of a word. However, the aim eventually is to make it round the circle with the rhythm repeated only once for each child.

Helpful hint

If the children need more time to think, increase the length of time by doubling each action (two pats on the knees... two claps... two clicks with each hand).

Ascending arms!

Age banding

7–11 (Years 3 to 6)

Aim

To remind the children that Jesus was raised up into heaven.

You will need

No equipment is needed.

How to play

Pair up each child with someone roughly the same size. Explain that one child in each pair is going to place their arms by their sides with their palms pressed against their thighs. Their partner is then going to place his or her hands over the first child's hands, thus holding them firmly on to that child's thighs. When you give the signal, the first child in each pair will push against their partner's hands, with the aim of lifting their own hands off their thighs. The second child will try to hold the first child's hands on to their thighs. The children need to apply a reasonable amount of pressure but nothing should hurt: if it does, they are trying too hard. The children keep up this pressure for about one minute.

When you say 'stop', the second child in each pair removes their hands and the first child completely relaxes their arms. The first child's arms should 'ascend' into the air. Ask the children to reverse roles and have another go. You can then swap children so that they try the experiment with different partners.

Helpful hints

- If there is an odd number of children, ask leaders to pair up with children who might otherwise be left without a partner.
- Sometimes it is helpful to demonstrate this experiment first.

*

THE COMING OF THE HOLY SPIRIT

Story reference: Acts 2:1–41

Flap the flame

Age banding
4–7 (Reception to Year 3)

Aim
To remind the children that the Holy Spirit appeared as flames on the heads of the believers.

You will need

No equipment is needed.

How to play
Ask the children to stand in a circle with one child in the middle. Show the children how to place their hands on their heads with their palms facing forwards, fingers stretched upwards and their thumbs interlinked. The aim is to make them look like flames on the children's heads. When the central child is looking at them, the children keep their 'flames' still. However, as soon as this child looks away, the children in the circle flap their flames as much as they wish. The task of the child in the centre is to catch a child in the circle flapping their flame.

The central child may need some advice on tactics, such as slowly turning one way and then quickly turning in the opposite direction. If a child is caught flapping, they swap with the child in the centre.

Helpful hint

This game can be played to reinforce other Bible stories by changing the action—for example, flapping cockerel wings for Peter's denial; quickly climbing a tree for Zacchaeus; using a sling for David and Goliath, and so on.

Fan the flame

Age banding
7–11 (Years 3 to 6)
All ages

Aim
To remind the children that the Holy Spirit appeared as flames on the heads of the believers.

You will need

Two pieces of A4 paper for each team (one piece needs to be cut or torn into a flame shape); a start and finish line (use tape, chalk, chairs or similar).

How to play
Divide the children into teams and ask them to stand behind the start line.

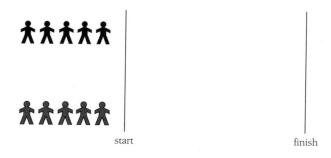

start   finish

Give each team a flame shape and another piece of A4 paper. Ask the teams to place their flames on the floor at the start line. Explain that each team member will take it in turns to use the other piece of paper to fan the flame over the finish line. When the flame crosses the finish line, the player will pick it up and run to pass it to the next team member. This player will then fan the flame, and so on, until each team member has completed the task. The first team to complete the task and sit down is the winner.

The children can fold or bend the A4 paper in any way they want to try to make the flame move more quickly. However, they must not touch the flame with the paper.

Helpful hints

- You may want to allow the children to blow the flames at the same time as creating the wind with the A4 paper.
- This game can also be used for Bible stories about fish: just cut a fish shape instead of a flame shape out of the paper.

*

PETER AND JOHN

Story reference: Acts 3:1–26

What I have, I give you!

Age banding

4–7 (Reception to Year 3)
All ages

Aim

To remind the children of Peter's response to the man who was
lame.

You will need

Two containers (long socks are ideal, but bags or boxes will
do—the children must not be able to see through or into
the containers); approximately 20 small items placed in
each container. The items need to be similar but need not
be identical—for example, a key could be placed in each
sock but it doesn't matter if the keys are different shapes.
Items could include paperclip, pen, rubber, lipstick, key, hair
bobble, 1p, 20p, £1, leaf, sweet, biscuit and so on.

How to play

Divide the children into two teams. Give one person in each team
a container. Explain that they are not allowed to put their hand
into the container until the leader says, 'Go'. The leader is going
to ask them to place their hand in the container and feel around

until they have found a particular item. When they think they have found the item, they must pull it out of the container and run to show the leader. If they are the first to do this, then their team earns one point. The item is then placed back into the container.

For example, say 'Can you find a paperclip? Go!' One child from each team places his or her hand in the container and feels around. A child finds the paperclip, pulls it out and runs to the leader. The paperclip is placed back in the container and the game repeated with a different object. The containers are passed to two different team members, who are asked to find a different item and bring it to the leader. This is repeated as many times as required, but at least until every team member has had a turn. The team with the most points at the end of the game is the winner.

Helpful hints

- You may want the children to say, 'What I have, I give you!' when they show the leader the item they have found, to remind them of the words that Peter spoke in the story.
- For younger children, use easier items, such as a pen, just one coin, a small birthday card, key, soft toy, roll of sticky tape and so on. If there are lots of children, have more teams and use more containers.

Walk and leap

Age banding
7–11 (Years 3 to 6)

Aim
To remind the children that God used Peter and John to heal the lame man at the temple.

You will need

No equipment is needed.

How to play

Teach the children the following actions to go with the words.

- **Lame man:** lying flat on the floor
- **Begging:** kneeling down with hands cupped together in the air
- **Walking:** walk round
- **Leaping:** leap round
- **Praising God:** put hands in the air and wave hands around
- **Peter and John:** grab nearest person and put arms round their shoulders

When the children have practised the actions, explain that they are going to begin by walking round the room. After a short while, the leader calls out an instruction. The children have to carry out the instruction as quickly as they can. If the leader then calls out a different word, they must immediately move on to the latest instruction.

For example, the children begin to walk round the room. The leader calls out 'Leaping' and the children leap around the room; the leader calls out 'Lame man' and the children lie flat on the floor; the leader calls out 'Begging' and the children kneel up to beg.

This is an active game so the instructions should be quick and snappy. The game can be played for fun or the last child to carry out each instruction could be called 'out' until a winner is found.

Helpful hint

If this game is going to be played to find an overall winner, it is good to have an area of the room marked off so that children who are out can move into that area. In this way, they can still join in and practise for the next game.

*

PHILIP AND THE ETHIOPIAN OFFICIAL

Story reference: Acts 8:26–40

Ready, steady, go!

Age banding
4–7 (Reception to Year 3)
All ages

Aim
To remind the children that Philip ran to catch up with the chariot in which the Ethiopian official was riding.

You will need

No equipment is needed.

How to play
Select one child to be the Ethiopian and ask them to stand at one end of the room. Ask all the other children to stand facing the Ethiopian at the opposite end of the room.

Ethiopian

Explain that when the Ethiopian shouts 'Red', the children must stand perfectly still. When he shouts 'Orange', they can walk towards him. When he shouts 'Green', the children can run towards him. If any child is seen to make the wrong movement—for example, makes any movement when 'Red' is called or runs on 'Orange'—that child is sent back to the start and continues the game from there. The first player to touch the Ethiopian takes his or her place and the game begins again. The game works best if the Ethiopian calls the colours quickly.

Helpful hint

It is best to play this game a few times with the leader as the Ethiopian. That way, the children get the hang of how to call out the colours and may also pick up a few tactics from the leader. It is also helpful if the leader is the one who sends children back to the start line, as it saves arguments.

Run!

Age banding

7–11 (Years 3 to 6)

Aim

To remind the children that Philip had to run to catch the chariot in which the Ethiopian was travelling.

You will need

No equipment is needed.

How to play

Ask all the children except one to stand in a circle and join hands loosely. Explain that the remaining player (child 1) is going to walk round the outside of the circle, suddenly pull apart two children's hands and shout 'Run!' The two children set off in opposite directions round the circle in a race to be the first back to their gap. At the same time, child 1 moves into the gap created when the two children set off running. Whichever child is first to arrive back at the gap high-fives child 1 and joins hands in the circle. The child who arrives second now walks round the circle and proceeds to separate two other children's hands.

Helpful hint

The children must hold hands very loosely, so that hands can be separated with ease.

---

*

THE EARLY CHURCH

Story reference: Acts 2:42–47

Working together

Age banding
4–7 (Reception to Year 3)
All ages

Aim
To remind the children that people in the early church worked together and shared everything they had.

You will need

Ten small pieces of paper with the numbers 1–10 written on them.

How to play
Split the children into two teams and appoint a leader for each team. Explain that you are going to ask all the children to wait outside the room while you hide the ten pieces of paper. Explain that, when you ask the children to come back into the room, they must find as many of the ten pieces of paper as they can. When they find a piece, they must give it to their leader. When all the pieces of paper have been found, the team will add up the numbers on the paper and the team with the highest score is the winner. The game can be repeated and the scores added up each time to give an overall winning team.

Helpful hint

Try to remember where you have hidden the pieces of paper: it is amazing how often one piece can't be found. After the first go, you may want a child to do the hiding.

All in this together

Age banding

7–11 (Years 3 to 6)

Aim

To help the children see the importance of working together, as people did in the early church.

You will need

No equipment is needed.

How to play

Split the children into teams of approximately 6–8. Ask each team to stand in a circle with the team members facing each other. Ask all the children to place one arm into the centre of the circle and take hold of someone's hand. Ask them to place their other hand into the middle and take hold of a different person's hand. The children should now be tangled together. The aim of the game is for the children to untangle themselves without letting go of each other. The children may loosen their grip to turn their hands in different directions, so that they don't get hurt, but they must always keep contact with the same hand. Some children may need to squat down so that others can step over their arms.

The children will need to talk to each other and share ideas. They will need to cooperate if they are to be successful. The game is over when a team is standing in a complete, untangled circle. Some team members may find they are facing outwards from the circle, which is fine.

Helpful hint

If possible, have a leader watching each team to make sure the children don't let go of hands, and also to give advice on how to detangle.

*

DORCAS

Story reference: Acts 9:32–43

Hanging out the clothes

Age banding
4–7 (Reception to Year 3)
All ages

Aim
To remind the children that Dorcas made clothes for people in need.

You will need

Scrap paper (paper destined for the recycling bin is ideal); chairs (two per team); string or wool (optional).

How to play
Split the children into small teams and give each team a few pieces of paper. Give each team a long piece of string and help them to attach it between two chairs (optional). Explain to the children that they are going to tear the paper to make clothes to hang on their washing line. (If a 'washing line' is not available, the children can lay their clothes on a table or on the floor.) Demonstrate to the children how to tear the paper to make an item of clothing such as a pair of trousers. Give the children a time limit to complete the task.

Sewing

Age banding

7–11 (Years 3 to 6)

Aim

To remind the children that Dorcas made clothes to help people in need.

You will need

No equipment is needed.

How to play

Ask all the children except two to stand in a circle, about an arm's width apart but with their hands by their sides. Choose one of the two remaining children to be the weaver and one the chaser. Explain that the weaver is going to weave in and out of the circle. This child does not have to go through every gap in order, but may run directly across the circle or through any gap he or she likes.

Whenever the weaver passes from the outside of the circle to the inside, the children on either side of the gap through which he or she passed join hands, thus 'sewing' up the gap. This gap can now not be passed through again. (When the weaver passes from the inside of the circle to the outside, nothing happens.)

The chaser remains on the outside of the circle at all times. His or her aim is to catch the weaver before the whole circle is sewn together. If the weaver is caught before the circle has been sewn up, a new game begins. The weaver joins the circle, the chaser becomes the weaver, and a new child is chosen to be the chaser. If the weaver is not caught, then both children are replaced by two others.

Helpful hint

After the first few turns, give the children time to discuss what tactics are useful in this game.

*

PAUL AND SILAS

Story reference: Acts 16:16–40

Earthquake

Age banding
4–7 (Reception to Year 3)
All ages

Aim
To remind the children that Paul and Silas were placed in prison for passing on the good news about Jesus, until an earthquake led to their release.

You will need

Pieces of A4 paper, each cut into four pieces; a plastic bowl to hold the pieces of paper; music CD and CD player (optional).

How to play
Ask the children to write their name on a piece of paper and fold it up. (Encourage only two folds.) Explain that, just as Paul and Silas passed on the good news about Jesus, they are going to pass their pieces of paper on to other people. When you say 'Go', the children begin to swap papers, and they continue to do this until you say 'Stop'. (If music is available, the children will continue to swap papers with as many others as possible while the music plays.) As soon as you ask them to stop (or the music stops), the children will

place the paper they are holding in the bowl and gather round it in a circle.

Choose one child to stand in the centre, holding the bowl. Ask all the children in the circle to join hands as if they are chained together. On your instruction, they are going to move their arms up and down as they count out loud from 1 to 10. On the word '10', the child in the middle will shout 'Earthquake!' loudly and will rattle the bowl up and down so that all the papers are scattered on the floor.

As soon as this happens, the children let go of each other's hands and move to collect a piece of paper. They quickly open the paper and, if it does not have their own name on it, they fold it back up, drop it back on the floor and move on to a different piece. The first child to find their own name shouts 'Freeze!' as loudly as they can. That child is the winner of the game. The children now collect one folded paper each (it doesn't need to be their own) and the swapping begins again.

Helpful hints

- It is a good idea to place a few folded pieces of paper, with no names on them, in the bowl alongside the ones with the children's names on. This will mean that there are always some spare papers to be found on the floor while the children are searching for their names.
- Make sure the names are readable: if possible, have a couple of leaders or older children who can read the names on the papers for any children who struggle with reading.

Chained!

Age banding
7–11 (Years 3 to 6)

Aim
To remind the children that Paul and Silas were held in chains in the prison cell before their miraculous escape.

You will need
A start and finish line (marked with tape or chairs).

How to play
Split the children into teams and ask them to line up behind a start line.

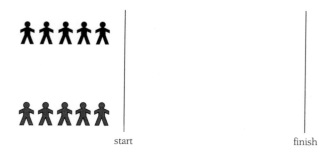

start   finish

Explain that the children are aiming to 'escape' across the finishing line by working together. Ask all the team members except one to squat down with their knees fully bent. Now ask those squatting down to 'chain' themselves together by placing their hands on the shoulders of the person in front. Explain that the spare player will act as the spokesperson. This player faces the team and must hold the hands of the first squatting player.

When you say 'Go', the children must remain chained together and must shuffle forward until the whole team has crossed the finish line. When the last team member crosses the line, they should shout 'Freed!' The spokesperson will need to give instructions so that the children can move forward in unison. If the chain is broken, the team must return to the start line and try again.

When the children have had a practice, you could encourage them to sing a worship chorus that they know well while they shuffle along to remind them that Paul and Silas praised God while they were chained.

Helpful hint

Once the children have mastered the game, you could change the action so that, instead of shuffling along, they do small jumps while chained together. The spokesperson should be changed each time a new race is attempted, so that different children are given a chance to lead.

*

SHIPWRECK

Story reference: Acts 27—28

Row, row!

Age banding

4–7 (Reception to Year 3)

Aim

To remind the children that Paul was shipwrecked on the island of Malta.

You will need
The tune for the well-known children's song 'Row, row, row your boat' (the children will probably know this song from school).

How to play

Split the children into pairs and ask each pair to sit on the floor facing each other with their feet touching. Ask them to take hold of each other's hands. (It doesn't matter if their knees are bent.) Ask if any of the children know the song 'Row, row, row your boat'. Sing it to the children and show them how to rock gently backwards and forwards. Explain that you are going to teach them some different words, relating to the story of Paul and the shipwreck. The words are as follows:

Chorus

Row, row, row your boat,
Quickly to the shore.
Can you find another friend?
Swap with them once more.

As the children sing, they should keep hold of each other's hands and rock backwards and forwards as if in a boat. On the word 'more', the children stand up and find another child to sit with. They then sing the next verse.

Verse 1

Row, row, row your boat,
Paul was in the sea.
Landed on an island
Where the natives gave them tea! (Yum yum)

The children rub their tummies and lick their lips when they say 'Yum yum'. The chorus is then repeated and the children swap with another friend before singing verse 2.

Verse 2

Row, row, row your boat,
Sickness was their fate.
God used Paul to heal them all.
Isn't God just great? (Hurray!)

The chorus is repeated again and the children swap with another friend. The song can be repeated as many times as needed.

Helpful hint

The children may enjoy thinking up another verse together with you that they could act out.

Man overboard!

Age banding
7–11 (Years 3 to 6)
All ages

Aim
To remind the children that Paul was shipwrecked on the island of Malta as he was transported to Rome.

You will need
No equipment is needed.

How to play
Explain the instructions below to the children.

- **Starboard:** children run to the right.
- **Port:** children run to the left.
- **Lifeboat deck:** children run to the back of the room.
- **Quarter deck:** children run to front of room.
- **Captain's coming:** children stand to attention and salute.
- **Climb the rigging:** children pretend to be climbing a ladder.
- **Man overboard:** child grabs another child. One of them kneels down on one knee while the other sits on the other knee.
- **Scrub the deck:** children get on knees, pretending to scrub the floor.
- **Brush the deck:** children pretend to brush up.
- **Clear the deck (only suitable in certain rooms):** children must get their feet off the floor by sitting on a chair, bench or similar.

Once the children have understood what action to perform for each instruction, the game begins. At first you may need to call out the instructions more slowly, but later one instruction after another can be called and the children will soon be out of breath. The idea is to keep the children moving.

Helpful hint

The children quickly get tired in this game, so, if numbers are large or space is limited, divide the children in half and let one half play while the others watch. To keep everyone involved, you could ask the watching children to be ready to kneel when you shout 'Man overboard' that so the children playing have to run to sit on one of the watching children's knees.

---

*

THE BIBLE

Story reference: The Bible

Old or New?

Age banding
4–7 (Reception to Year 3)
All ages

Aim
To remind the children that the Bible is divided into two parts: the Old and New Testaments.

You will need

Two pieces of paper with 'Old Testament' written on one and 'New Testament' written on the other; A4 paper cut into lots of small pieces, approximately 2cm x 2cm (exact size is not important).

How to play
Place the two signs in different parts of the room. Place a pile of small pieces of paper next to the signs. Talk to the children about the Old and New Testaments, making sure they know that the Old Testament is about the time before Jesus was born and the New Testament is about Jesus' life and the time shortly after he returned to heaven.

Explain that you are going to say the names of lots of different people in the Bible. When you say a name, you want the children to decide if they think the person would be found in the Old Testament part of the Bible or the New Testament part. When they have decided, they need to go and stand beside the correct sign. When every child has decided on their answer, tell the children the correct answer and ask all the children at the right sign to collect a piece of paper. Now ask the children to move back into the middle and give them a different Bible character to decide upon.

Each time a child answers correctly, they receive a piece of paper. They need to keep these safe, as the child with the most pieces at the end is the winner.

Bible characters could include the following (muddle up the two lists when calling out the names):

- **Old Testament:** Abraham, Noah, Jonah, Moses, Solomon, Adam, David, Isaiah, Eve, Goliath, Samuel, Ruth, Esther, Jacob, Aaron, Samson, Elisha, Rebecca, Daniel, Hannah
- **New Testament:** Jesus, Peter, Matthew, John, Lydia, Paul, Anna, Judas, Mark, Luke, Mary, Joanna, James

If you want to make the game more complicated, you could have another section for names that appear in both the Old and New Testaments, such as Joseph or Saul. Alternatively, you could include names that don't appear in the Bible at all, such as Shaun, Charlotte, Rose, Kelly, Richard, Lauren, Angela and so on. A variation on the game would be to use books of the Bible, to see if children know which books are in the Old and New Testaments.

Helpful hint

When cutting up the small pieces of paper, cut a few sheets at a time and don't worry if they are not the same size. It is the number collected that matters. If possible, have an adult leader or older child standing next to each pile of paper to help the children collect them.

Fizz... buzz

Age banding

7–11 (Years 3 to 6)

Aim

To help the children learn the number of books in the Bible.

You will need
No equipment is needed.

How to play

See if the children are aware of how many books are in the Old Testament and the New Testament and in the Bible as a whole (Old Testament: 39; New Testament: 27; Total: 66).

Ask the children to sit in a circle, facing inwards. Explain that the children are going to count up to 27 (the number of books in the New Testament). Someone will start by saying '1', the next child will say '2' and so on. They are going to take it in turns to say consecutive numbers until 27 is reached. However, there is a twist! If the number is in the three times table, instead of the number the child will say 'fizz'. If the number is in the five times table, the child will say 'buzz'. If the number is in both the three and five times tables, the child will say 'fizz buzz'.

You may want to run through the game just doing the three times table first, using the word 'fizz'. Once the children are ready to add in the five times table, the order will be: 1, 2, fizz, 4, buzz, fizz, 7, 8, fizz, buzz, 11, fizz, 13, 14, fizz-buzz, 16, 17, fizz, 19, buzz, fizz, 22, 23, fizz, buzz, 26, fizz.

The game usually causes great hilarity. The aim is to eventually get up to 27 without a mistake. You may like to go back to the beginning every time a mistake is made, or allow for mistakes if it proves too difficult. When the children have mastered going up to 27, they can then try reaching 39 (the number of books in the Old Testament). If the children manage this, they can try the ultimate challenge of 66 (the whole Bible).

Helpful hints

- You may like to hand out Bibles at the beginning of this game so that the children can use the contents page to count the books for themselves.
- For younger children, write the three and five times tables on a piece of paper before you attempt the game.

Also from BRF/Barnabas

PARACHUTE FUN FOR EVERYONE

50 playchute activities for telling Bible stories, teaching and worship

Renita Boyle

Playchutes are multi-coloured, multi-age and multi-fun from the moment they appear from their bags to the moment they are packed awy. They are increasingly valued as a tool in Christian teaching and worship activities, including storytelling, songs, prayers, praise, reflection and games, as they naturally encourage many of the values at the heart of the Christian faith.

Parachute Fun for Everyone is packed with 50 pick-and-mix activity ideas to use with children, mixed-age groups including adults, and those with special needs. Guidance is given as to energy levels, suitable age groups and necessary accessories.

Many of the activities are adapted from well-known parachute and circle games long in use. What makes them valuable beyond the fun factor is the opportunity for spiritual growth as you explore and respond to their themes together.

ISBN 978 1 84101 702 0   £6.99
Available from your local Christian bookshop or, in case of difficulty, direct from BRF: please visit www.brfonline.org.uk.

ENCYCLOPEDIA OF BIBLE CRAFTS

187 fun-filled, easy-to-do craft activities for children

Laurie Castañeda

Children love doing craft activities—and children's leaders love crafts that connect children to Bible truths! This bumper collection of creative, fun-filled and easy-to-do Bible crafts is designed to inspire and enthuse leaders and children alike as they explore the Bible together.

Each tried-and-tested craft is designed to fit into any Bible-based children's work programme, whether that's on a Sunday, midweek, or a one-off special event. Every single book of the Bible is covered, with crafts to illustrate many key Bible passages. The crafts are easy to prepare, easy to do and require very little equipment or materials.

Alongside the craft activities you will also find:

- An age guide for each craft
- A Bible reference
- A Bible point
- 'You will need' list
- Handy hints
- Step-by-step instructions
- Teaching point

ISBN 978 0 85746 217 6   £12.99
Available from your local Christian bookshop or, in case of difficulty, direct from BRF: please visit www.brfonline.org.uk

Also from BRF/Barnabas

PAPER PLATE BIBLE CRAFTS

58 easy-to-do ideas for 5–7s

Anita Reith Stohs

Paper Plate Bible Crafts is a great resource for fun crafts that teach favourite Bible stories in any setting.

Fast, inexpensive and readily available, paper plates easily become masks, mobiles, puppets and plaques. The finished crafts are an ingenious way to reinforce Bible stories and themes.

The book includes 58 tried and tested ideas for 5–7s, each with simple templates and easy-to-follow instructions. Alongside the paper plate, each craft uses basic, everyday materials such as card, felt-tipped pens, scissors and glue and can be completed as suggested or adapted to suit the needs and skills of the children.

Each craft idea includes:

- Key Bible story reference
- Full equipment list
- Easy-to-follow instructions
- Simple discussion starters
- Alternative ideas for making the craft
- Illustration of the finished craft

ISBN 978 0 85746 261 9   £7.99
Available from your local Christian bookshop or, in case of difficulty, direct from BRF: please visit www.brfonline.org.uk

Enjoyed

this book?

Write a review—we'd love to hear what you think.
Email: reviews@brf.org.uk

Keep up to date—receive details of our new books as they happen.
Sign up for email news and select your interest groups at:
www.brfonline.org.uk/findoutmore/

Follow us on Twitter @brfonline

By post—to receive new title information by post (UK only), complete the form below and post to: BRF Mailing Lists, 15 The Chambers, Vineyard, Abingdon, Oxfordshire, OX14 3FE

Your Details
Name _____
Address_____
_____
Town/City _____ Post Code _____
Email_____

Your Interest Groups (*Please tick as appropriate)	
☐ Advent/Lent	☐ Messy Church
☐ Bible Reading & Study	☐ Pastoral
☐ Children's Books	☐ Prayer & Spirituality
☐ Discipleship	☐ Resources for Children's Church
☐ Leadership	☐ Resources for Schools

Support your local bookshop
Ask about their new title information schemes.